OSPREY
MILITARY

CAMPAIGN SERIES   18

W9-CRB-582

GUADALCANAL 1942

GENERAL EDITOR DAVID G. CHANDLER

OSPREY
MILITARY

CAMPAIGN SERIES

18

GUADALCANAL 1942

THE MARINES STRIKE BACK

JOSEPH N. MUELLER

◀ *These Marines evacu-*
ating a casualty from the
front are part of the 2nd
Marine Division. The
terrain in the picture
indicates that it was taken
along the coast near
Kokumbona sometime in
the January 1943 push.
The strain caused by
jungle warfare on
Guadalcanal is evident in
these men's faces. The
Marine being taken out on
the stretcher is being
taken to a battalion aid
station, which operated
close to the battle area.
(USMC 53444)

▼ *The rains on Guadalcanal frequently turned the camps into quagmires. Without proper drainage, the areas held standing water for days at a time. Clothing and canvas rarely dried and eventually rotted; weapons rusted and malarial mosquitoes bred, causing the spread of disease. In spite of all these conditions, life on Guadalcanal went on. (USMC 74085)*

For a catalogue of all books published by Osprey Military, please write to:

The Marketing Manager,
Consumer Catalogue Department, Osprey Publishing Ltd,
59 Grosvenor Street, London W1X 9DA.

First published in 1992 by Osprey Publishing Ltd.
59 Grosvenor Street, London W1X 9DA

ISBN 1-85532-253-6

Produced by DAG Publications Ltd for Osprey Publishing Ltd. Colour bird's eye view illustrations by Cilla Eurich. Cartography by Micromap. *Wargaming Guadalcanal* by Bob Cordery. Wargames consultant Duncan Macfarlane. Typeset by Ronset Typesetters, Darwen, Lancashire. Mono camerawork by M&E Reproductions, North Fambridge, Essex. Printed and bound in Hong Kong.

CONTENTS

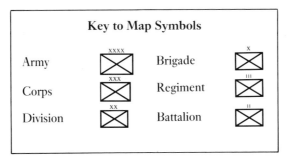

Key to Map Symbols

Army   Brigade

Corps   Regiment

Division   Battalion

The Strategic Situation, July-August 1942

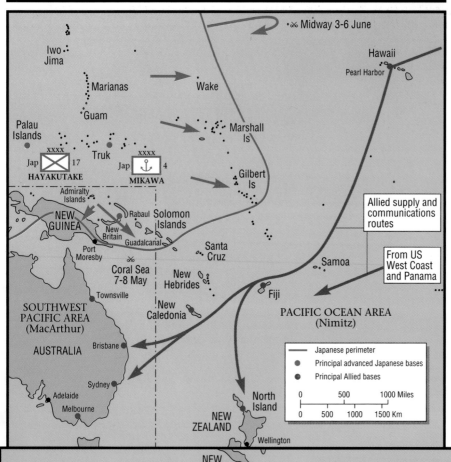

Midway 3-6 June

Iwo Jima

Hawaii
Pearl Harbor

Marianas
Wake

Guam

Palau Islands
Truk
Marshall Is

XXXX
Jap 17
HAYAKUTAKE

XXXX
Jap 4
MIKAWA

Gilbert Is

Admiralty Islands

NEW GUINEA
Rabaul
New Britain
Solomon Islands

Guadalcanal
Santa Cruz

Port Moresby

Coral Sea 7-8 May
New Hebrides

Samoa

Fiji

Townsville

SOUTHWEST PACIFIC AREA (MacArthur)

New Caledonia

PACIFIC OCEAN AREA (Nimitz)

AUSTRALIA
Brisbane

Sydney

Adelaide

Melbourne

North Island

NEW ZEALAND
Wellington

Allied supply and communications routes

From US West Coast and Panama

Japanese perimeter
● Principal advanced Japanese bases
● Principal Allied bases

0   500   1000 Miles
0   500   1000   1500 Km

The Japanese takeover of Guadalcanal represented the farthest limit of their Pacific advance in the Second World War. With bases established throughout New Guinea, the Bismarck Archipelago and the Solomon Islands, they began to pose a serious threat to the communications lifeline that ran between Hawaii and Australia.

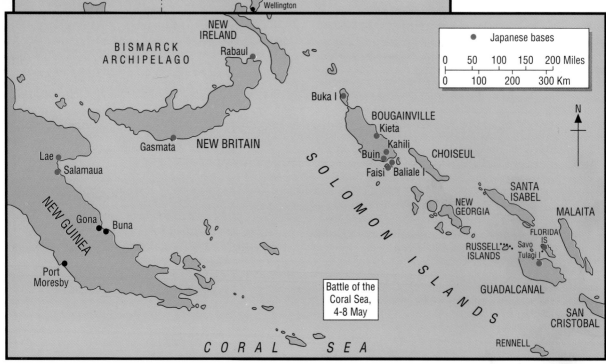

NEW IRELAND

BISMARCK ARCHIPELAGO
Rabaul

● Japanese bases

0   50   100   150   200 Miles
0   100   200   300 Km

Buka I

BOUGAINVILLE
Kieta

Kahili
Buin
CHOISEUL
Faisi Baliale I

Gasmata NEW BRITAIN

Lae
Salamaua

SANTA ISABEL

NEW GEORGIA

MALAITA

NEW GUINEA

Gona Buna

FLORIDA IS
RUSSELL Savo
ISLANDS Tulagi I

Port Moresby

SOLOMON ISLANDS

Battle of the Coral Sea, 4-8 May

GUADALCANAL

SAN CRISTOBAL

RENNELL

CORAL SEA

N

THE ORIGINS OF THE CAMPAIGN

Guadalcanal was the first American amphibious counteroffensive of the Second World War. It was on this virtually unheard of island that the Americans shattered the myth of Japanese invincibility in the Pacific. Although the Battles of Midway and the Coral Sea are described as turning-point battles, it was at Guadalcanal that the Japanese war machine was ground to a halt. After Guadalcanal there were no other advances made by the Japanese in the Pacific.

The Battle for Guadalcanal was a unique battle for many reasons. Both the American and Japanese forces fought at the farthest end of their supply lines. The battle itself would be among the longest in duration of the Pacific campaign. It would take six months of fierce and savage fighting, testing the endurance of both sides, before the Japanese were driven off the island; the climate and terrain, which were equally harsh, proved an enemy to both sides. Ship losses off Guadalcanal, comparable to those suffered later off the Philippines and Okinawa, were so great that the waters along the north coast of Guadalcanal would become known as 'Iron Bottom Sound' – a name that continues to this day.

The burden of the conflict was endured by the United States Navy and the Marine Corps. However the army forces soon joined in and saw their fair share of combat as well. The troops first to experience the cruel realities of jungle warfare were the Marines of the newly formed 1st Marine Division. This division was deployed from the east coast of the United States to Wellington, New Zealand, where it was to complete its training; the Division was not expected to see combat until after January 1943.

The movement of the Marines overseas was accomplished without incident. The advance echelon, consisting primarily of Major General Vandegrift's divisional headquarters and the 5th Marine Regiment under Colonel Leroy P. Hunt, with the 2nd Battalion, 11th Marine Regiment and twelve other unit detachments, arrived in Wellington on 14 June 1942. Training and camp sites had been selected before their arrival by a small group of officers working in conjunction with the New Zealand military. The camp sites were ideally chosen and were in close proximity to good training areas on the south-western tip of North Island.

The Japanese on the other hand were operating to a different time table. Their advance took them to the North Coast of New Guinea and into the Admiralty Islands. They continued their unopposed advance into the Solomon Islands and pushed south, seizing Tulagi and Guadalcanal, there to begin construction of an airfield.

As these events were occurring on the local level, strategic planning commenced on the American Joint Chiefs of Staff level. The Joint Chiefs were aware that the Japanese advance in the Pacific threatened the communications lifeline to Australia. Furthermore, American bases that lay in the path of the Japanese advance would be endangered. The Joint Chiefs concluded that an American offensive in the Pacific was now a matter of necessity.

Once it was determined that the Japanese were constructing an airfield on Guadalcanal, the 1st Marine Division was given the mission of seizing that island. The date set for the amphibious assault was 1 August 1942, nearly eight months to the day after the Japanese attacked Pearl Harbor.

THE OPPOSING PLANS

The Japanese Plan

From 7 December 1941 to 7 May 1942, the Japanese advanced with seeming precision, sweeping through east Asia, the Indies and a large portion of Melanesia. They overran the Philippines, Wake Island, Guam and Singapore. As their seemingly unstoppable advance continued, they seized Rabaul on the island of New Britain on 23 January 1943. They thereby acquired a key objective. Rabaul was just 1,200 nautical miles from their bases in the Palau Islands and 640 nautical miles from their base at Truk. It could easily be defended and converted to a bastion from which future offensive operations could be launched. It also had the best harbour in the region and excellent terrain for the construction of airfields.

From Rabaul the Japanese could dominate New Guinea and the Solomon Islands. Once these two areas could be controlled, the Japanese could sever the communications lifeline between Hawaii and Australia.

In March 1942, the Japanese seized Bougainville in the Northern Solomons. From there they proceeded down the Solomons to the centre of British Government, Tulagi. After seizing operational bases on the northern coast of New Guinea

▼Officers and petty officer of the 3rd Kure Special Landing Force who seized Tulagi and Gavutu on 3 May. This picture was taken prior to the invasion, at their base in Japan. The majority of the men in this picture were killed between 7 and 9 August in action against the Marines. (USMC)

and in the Solomon Islands, they attacked Tulagi on 1 May 1942. Unable to defend Tulagi adequately, the British withdrew from the area. Then, on 3 May 1942, the 2nd and 3rd Companies of the Kure Special Landing Force, supported by a small naval force, made an unopposed landing on Tulagi and Gavutu.

The operation did not go unhindered. The next day, dive-bombers and torpedo planes from the American aircraft carriers *Enterprise* and *Yorktown* raided Tulagi sinking the destroyer *Kikutsuki* and damaging other ships. This attack was the opening phase of the Battle of the Coral Sea. In that battle, the Americans turned back a large Japanese task force that was advancing on Port Moresby, New Guinea. After the Battle of the Coral Sea, the Japanese commander at Rabaul advised his subordinates that the battle had depleted Japanese naval forces in the area. He further advised that supply lines to Lae and Tulagi were in great danger. His greatest concern was for the New Guinea area.

Tulagi did not receive much attention. After landing, the small 380 man Japanese force began improving existing facilities by building seaplane bases on Tulagi and Gavutu. Once this was accomplished, they began generally exploring their new conquests. For about a month, no immediate steps were taken to develop bases in the area. Then, in late June 1942, survey parties went ashore at Lunga Point on the north coast of the

▲ *The Japanese destroyer Kikutsuki participated in the Japanese invasion of Tulagi on 3 May 1942. She gave fire support to the Kure Special Landing Force that made an unopposed landing. On the following day she was* sunk in an air raid by pilots from the American aircraft carrier Yorktown. *In October 1943 she was raised and used as a floating repair ship by the 34th Construction Battalion. (National Archives 80-G-89212)*

big island of Guadalcanal. There they explored the possibility of building an airfield. By mid-July construction had started, with completion estimated by mid-August.

According to Japanese documents captured later, the objective of capturing Tulagi and building an airfield on Guadalcanal was to protect their flank while carrying out their main attack on Port Moresby, New Guinea. The secondary objective was to secure a favourable base of operations to move south through New Caledonia to attack Australia. This attack was to take place after the capture of New Guinea.

The American Plan

The American plan for the invasion of Guadalcanal began with inter-service rivalries. After the Battle of the Coral Sea, in early May 1942, General Douglas MacArthur, Commander of the Southwest Pacific Forces (CINCSWPA), realized that the Japanese would eventually attempt to sever the lines of communication between Hawaii and

Australia. He felt that a Japanese attack on New Guinea was inevitable. To prevent such an attack he wanted to take the offensive against the Japanese in the New Britain–New Ireland areas. An attack of this nature would force the Japanese out of the region and back to Truk. MacArthur's plan found favour with General George C. Marshall, US Army Chief of Staff. However, MacArthur did not have the resources available to launch such an offensive. Further, he had no troops under his command that had any experience of amphibious warfare.

Simultaneously, Admiral Chester W. Nimitz, Commander in Chief Pacific Fleet (CINCPAC)

and Pacific Ocean Area (CINCPOA), was contemplating a strike on Tulagi, a plan that found favour with Admiral Ernest J. King, Chief of Naval Operations, Joint Chiefs of Staff. Originally, Nimitz had advocated the taking of Tulagi with a Marine Raider Battalion, but the concept was rejected by King, who felt the force was not suitable. However, King felt that the immediate objectives should be in the Solomon and Santa Cruz Islands, with the ultimate objective in the New Guinea and New Britain area.

The Operations Division of the War Department (OPD), did not favour the Navy plan to attack and occupy Tulagi and move progressively against Rabaul: they felt that the quick strike at Rabaul had the most merit. Once Rabaul was taken the Japanese would be driven from the area and other positions could be isolated.

To complicate the issue further, neither side in the debate could agree on an operational commander. The Navy felt that MacArthur might

▼ Joint Chiefs of Staff during the Guadalcanal campaign. From left to right: Lieutenant General Henry H. Arnold, Admiral William D. Leahy, Admiral Ernest J. King and the Chairman, General George C. Marshall. It was inter-service rivalries between King and Marshall that caused some friction during the planning stages of the campaign. (National Archives)

unnecessarily expose its carriers to land based aircraft while they would be operating in restricted waters with limited aircraft carrier capability. They also felt Tulagi should be taken first to lessen the Japanese danger, at the same time establishing a base in the Solomons for future operations. This would allow a build-up of naval power for future operations. The Navy concluded that command should be through Nimitz, to his subordinate, Vice Admiral Robert L. Ghormley, Commander South Pacific Area and South Pacific Force (COMSO-PAC). MacArthur objected strenuously. He felt he was the logical choice for command since the amphibious objectives were in his area. However he lacked the ground troops to initiate an amphibious mission.

Between 29 June and 2 July 1942, the Joint Chiefs of Staff met and came up with a compromise plan. It called for Admiral Ghormley to command the Tulagi portion of the upcoming offensive; thereafter General MacArthur would command the advance to Rabaul. The American Navy with the Marine Corps would attack, seize and defend Tulagi, Guadalcanal and the surrounding area, while MacArthur made a parallel advance on New Guinea. Both drives would aim at Rabaul. The boundary between Southwest Pacific Area and the South Pacific Area was moved to reflect this, and South Pacific Forces were given the go-ahead to initiate planning. Admiral King had not waited for the final approval: on 25 June 1942 he notified Nimitz to alert Ghormley to start planning. Ghormley in turn contacted Major General Alexander A. Vandegrift, the Commanding General, 1st Marine Division (reinforced), that his division would spearhead the amphibious assault, scheduled to take place on 1 August 1942.

For General Vandegrift the problems were just beginning. He had not expected to go into combat until after January 1943. Only a third of his division was at Wellington; a third was still at sea; and the other third had been detached to garrison Samoa. In little less than a month Vandegrift would have to prepare operational and logistical plans, unload part of his ships, reload for combat, sail from Wellington to the Fiji Islands for an amphibious rehearsal, and then sail to the Solomon Islands to drive out the Japanese.

To make the amphibious assault, the cargo that had been loaded in America would have to be reconfigured into a combat load. This in itself would pose a difficult set of problems and take place in New Zealand at Aotea Quay, a confined area that could only berth five ships at a time. To make bad matters worse, two other events compounded the misery. First, the dock workers went on strike so that the Marines had do all the stevedore work themselves. Next came the rains, which were steady for almost the entire period and were driven by a cold, persistent wind. The Marines worked around the clock in three eight-hour shifts, and the docks offered no protection from the weather. Space was adequate for stacking cargo, but it was left unprotected. The net result was the loss of food and clothing, which had been packaged in cardboard cartons that virtually dissolved. Morale of the Marines also suffered while working in such conditions – and, to make matters even worse, an influenza epidemic broke out. Once the combat loading task was completed, it was discovered that there was not enough room for all the motor transport to go back aboard: nearly all one-ton vehicles and below were put aboard, but 75 per cent of the heavier prime movers had to be left behind.

In addition to all this, Vandegrift would have to gather intelligence on an amphibious objective that most people had never heard of nor been to. Information on Guadalcanal in the summer of 1942 ranged from sketchy to completely unreliable. There were two main sources of information available to the Division's intelligence officer, Lieutenant Colonel Frank B. Goettge. The first source was obtainable from former residents of the area, who were now scattered throughout New Zealand and Australia. Goettge set up an extensive interview programme to gain as much information as possible. The second source of intelligence was from maps and hydrographic charts of the region. Unfortunately, these proved to be virtually nonexistent.

The most useful source of information came from aerial photos taken by Lieutenant Colonel Merril B. Twining and Major William B. Kean on

17 July 1942. The flight was made in an Army B-17 bomber based at Port Moresby, New Guinea, but it was cut short when three Japanese float planes were observed taking off from the Tulagi area to attack the B-17. The aerial photographs did not clearly identify the Japanese airfield, but they did give an excellent view of the north coast of Guadalcanal and the Tulagi area. It would be maps made from these photographs of the northern coast that the Marines would use for the majority of the campaign.

Realizing the enormity of the task ahead. Vandegrift asked for an extension of the invasion date. He was given one week: the amphibious assault would take place on 7 August 1942. There would be no further postponements, for the Japanese had most of the airfield completed.

With logistical preparations completed so far as time permitted, General Vandegrift issued the tactical orders. The grouping of the Marines for the operation was based on intelligence estimates of Japanese forces in the area. It was estimated that of the 8,400 Japanese believed in the area, 1,400 were on Tulagi and its neighbouring islands. The remaining 7,000 were thought to be on Guadalcanal, but this later turned out to be an erroneous estimate; only about half that number were there.

It was anticipated that Tulagi would be the more difficult of the two amphibious objectives. The Marines going ashore there would have to make a direct assault against a small, defended island. To protect the flanks of the Marines landing on Tulagi, it was decided first to seize key points overlooking Tulagi on nearby Florida Island. Later in the day, Gavutu, Tanambogo and the other smaller islands would be taken. With their seizure, the Tulagi portion of the operation would be completed.

▶*Lieutenant General Harukichi Hyakutake, Commanding General of the Japanese Seventeenth Army, was assigned the mission of recapturing Guadalcanal. Preoccupied with the capture of New Guinea, he did not grasp the seriousness of the Guadalcanal battle until it was too late, and his piecemeal attacks were defeated by the Americans in detail. (National Archives)*

THE OPPOSING COMMANDERS

The Japanese Commanders

Japanese troops in the Solomon Islands in the summer of 1942 constituted a force to be concerned with, but were not numerically superior, while the Japanese command structure was disjointed and plagued with a lack of cooperation between the Army and Navy.

Army forces in the area centred around the Japanese Seventeenth Army under the command of Lieutenant General Harukichi Hayakutake, who was preoccupied with the conquest of New Guinea.

The naval commander tasked with defence of the area was Vice Admiral Gunichi Mikawa, a seasoned officer who had commanded the escort for Admiral Nagumo's carrier force from Pearl Harbor to the Indian Ocean. Mikawa was in command of the 4th Fleet (Inner South Seas Force), not a large force and composed of either middle-aged or older ships.

Although Mikawa was tasked with defence of the area, he did not have control over the air units at Rabaul. They were controlled by Vice Admiral Nishizo Tuskahara, Commander of the 11th Air Fleet. Mikawa was justifiably concerned with the command and control measures utilized by the Japanese forces in the area. He was also disturbed by the lack of preparedness on the part of forces in the Solomons. The members of his staff thought he was an alarmist.

▲ *Vice Admiral Gunichi Mikawa, Imperial Japanese Navy, was the architect of the Battle of Savo Island. This battle was the worst defeat suffered by the American Navy since Pearl Harbor.* *Mikawa was appalled by the lack of a cohesive command in the Solomon Islands area. By his staff he was considered an alarmist. (Naval Historical Center)*

The American Commanders

For the Guadalcanal campaign the American command was set up under Admiral Nimitz, with Admiral Ghormley as Commander of the South Pacific Area (COMSOPAC) and the South Pacific Force. Ghormley would be in overall command of the operation, code named 'Watchtower'. Ghorm-ley, in turn, would appoint Vice Admiral Frank J. Fletcher as commander of the entire task force. This naval task force, designated an Expeditionary Force, was made up of two groups: the aircraft carriers constituted the Air Support Force, under Rear Admiral Leigh Noyes; other warships and the

◀ *General Vandegrift, Commanding General, 1st Marine Division, Guadalcanal. This portrait depicts him some time after Guadalcanal when he became Commandant of the Marine Corps. The senior, or topmost, ribbon on his uniform, is the Congressional Medal of Honor, America's highest award for valour; it was presented to him for his skills as commanding general on Guadalcanal. (USMC A413197)*

▶ *Vice Admiral Robert L. Ghormley, Commander of the South Pacific area and South Pacific Force (COMSOPAC) was in command of the Guadalcanal phase of the Joint Chiefs of Staff plan. Ghormley was a competent leader and planner; however, he never left his command centre at Noumea, New Caledonia, to get a first-hand account of the fighting. (Naval Historical Center)*

transports were organized as the Amphibious Force, under Rear Admiral Richmond K. Turner. Major General Alexander A. Vandegrift would command the Marines as part of the Landing Force.

This command set up, which placed Vandegrift's Marines under the Amphibious Force commander, stemmed back to an earlier era. The Navy felt the Marines were an extension of the forces afloat and still connected to the Navy. The Navy would therefore not only designate the Landing Force Objective, but the manner in which the land campaign would be prosecuted. The Marines, knowing the intricacies of an amphibious assault, were not overjoyed with this relationship. They believed that, once they were ashore and firmly established, command should be transferred

from the Navy: the Marine commander ashore could then best control the battlefield.

Rear Admiral V. A. C. Crutchley, Royal Australian Navy, would provide the anti-aircraft protection and the naval gunfire support for the operation. His forces were detached from Mac-Arthur to assist in the operation.

To assist Admiral Ghormley in any dealings with the US Army, Major General Millard F. Harmon, Commanding General US Army Forces South Pacific Area (COMGENSOPAC), was assigned to his command. Further, General Harmon would also be responsible for the administration and supply of Army units in the South Pacific Area. This, then, was the command that propelled the American forces towards the amphibious objective area.

▲Vice Admiral Frank J. Fletcher was the commander of the naval task force at the invasion of Guadalcanal. His decision to withdraw the aircraft carriers on 9 August caused disastrous consequences in the early stages of the campaign, for it left the Marines ashore virtually unsupported and without adequate supplies. (National Archives)

◄En route to Guadalcanal, Rear Admiral Richmond K. Turner goes over the movement to objective area with Major General Vandegrift. Turner was a brilliant amphibious planner; however, his relationship with Vandegrift was sometimes strained by philosophical differences. Turner was the commander of the amphibious task force and was senior to Vandegrift, who was commander of the landing force. (Naval Historical Center)

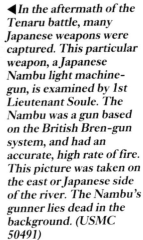

◀In the aftermath of the Tenaru battle, many Japanese weapons were captured. This particular weapon, a Japanese Nambu light machine-gun, is examined by 1st Lieutenant Soule. The Nambu was a gun based on the British Bren-gun system, and had an accurate, high rate of fire. This picture was taken on the east or Japanese side of the river. The Nambu's gunner lies dead in the background. (USMC 50491)

◀A Marine tests a captured Japanese flame-thrower on Guadalcanal. Neither side used this type of weapon in the campaign, but it was to be used quite effectively by the Marines against the Japanese in the later Pacific campaigns. (USMC 50046)

◀Captured Japanese weapons. The Marine in this picture is holding a Japanese Arisaka Model 38 bolt-action rifle. The rifle fired a 6.5mm (.25-cal) bullet which was inferior to the .30/06 Springfield rifle used by the Marines. The machine-gun mounted on the tripod is a Model 92 heavy machine-gun, which fired a 7.7mm bullet. It was serviced by a crew who could carry it into battle assembled with the pole carrying handles seen attached to the tripod legs. The weapons in the foreground are Model 99 Nambu light machine-guns; they fired a 7.7mm bullet and were extremely effective weapons. (USMC 108575)

THE OPPOSING FORCES

Guadalcanal would set the tone for the future campaigns of the war in the Pacific – not just one battle of quick duration, but a series of land, air and sea battles 'slugged out' along a narrow coastal belt, in restricted waterways and in the air space over Guadalcanal.

The reason why the campaign was to be so prolonged was that neither side would be able to mass its forces at a critical juncture to obtain a decisive victory. The Japanese and the Americans were operating at the farthest points of their supply lines. The Americans were hampered further by the fact that the bulk of their Pacific Fleet (with the exception of their aircraft carriers) had been sunk at Pearl Harbor, and that they were fighting a two-ocean war. The eventual outcome would be decided by the dogged determination of the American forces committed to the campaign and the release of critically needed supplies and equipment – coupled with luck.

The Japanese Forces

Initially, the Japanese were successful in the early naval battles. With the Battle of Savo Island (8-9 August) they achieved a great naval victory that severely crippled the American Navy's ability to support the operations ashore and in the waters surrounding Guadalcanal. And initially, with their land based fighters they also were able to control the air space overhead. Their ground forces were seasoned fighters and had achieved notable military successes up to Guadalcanal.

Japanese soldiers were masters of camouflage and reputably masters of jungle warfare. Their artillery was accurate, but not mobile enough for the type of jungle warfare engaged in. The tanks they used were also inadequate. The tactics the Japanese used, or were forced to use, were not conducive to success. For the most part, they attempted to conceal the movement of their forces in the jungle of Guadalcanal. This of course restricted their movements considerably. Much of the terrain they traversed was rain forest with few footpaths to travel on. Communications in the jungle were poor, and supplies were limited to what could be manpacked. Couple all of these disadvantages with a tropical disease factor second to none and you have a formula for disaster. Of the 21,500 casualties suffered by the Japanese in the campaign, 9,000 were to die of tropical diseases. By the end of the campaign the Japanese would be reduced to scavenging their food from the jungle.

As for the Japanese soldier, he was hardy and more than likely had some prior combat experience. He was tenacious, and subscribed to the code of 'bushido', or warrior, preferring death to capture. As he was subject to privations and stern discipline, those who became his prisoners were shown little mercy.

The Japanese Army was fairly well organized at the regimental level and below, but rarely did it operate at a divisional level. It consistently underestimated the capabilities of its enemies, a course of action that would prove disastrous on Guadalcanal. It also lacked security consciousness, and many of its soldiers carried detailed diaries into combat. Small unit leadership was not stressed: the running of the command and its employment was centred around the officers and senior sergeants.

The Japanese Navy on the other hand was an efficient organization. Tactically it could operate by day as well as by night. It was a disciplined aggressive force that carried out its assigned tasks without hesitation, using its weapons systems with deadly efficiency. Most notable was the infamous 'Long Lance' 24-inch diameter torpedo, which was used in conjunction with naval gunfire to

This Second lieutenant of the Imperial Japanese Army is armed with a Taisho 14 (1925) 8mm pistol. (Shirley Mallinson)

inflict maximum damage upon American warships.

The most serious failing of the Japanese Navy was its inability to exploit its successes. Time and time again throughout the naval campaign the Japanese achieved a tactical victory and then departed. By exploiting their successes they could have achieved a strategic victory.

In the air, the Japanese had clearly achieved a technological masterpiece with the zero fighter. This aircraft, with its lightweight construction and high rate of climb, could outmanoeuvre any American plane on Guadalcanal, but its diving capability was poor and it was not well suited to absorb punishment inflicted on it in aerial combat. Another disadvantage the Japanese had in the air was the amount of time they could spend over Guadalcanal: their time of flight and fuel consumption meant that their air missions were extremely restricted.

The American Forces

The American troops who invaded Guadalcanal were for the most part untried volunteers. The bulk of the initial combat forces were from the newly formed 1st Marine Division, of which only the advance elements were in Wellington at the time the decision was made for the amphibious assault on Guadalcanal. The remainder were to arrive just prior to embarkation.

The majority of the equipment that the Marines had was First World War vintage. Although it was time tested, in many cases it was either antiquated or worn out; either way, it was generally not suited for conditions on Guadalcanal.

Medical technology, although better than the Japanese, was inadequate in coping with the jungle diseases, primarily malaria. Communications were a problem, but since the Marines had mostly internal lines, these were not as severe as the problems experienced by the Japanese.

The tactics used by the Marines to encounter the Japanese were basic. Preparing to seize and then defend the airfield, they held the key terrain features that were encompassed by the Lunga Perimeter. On these they created strongpoints, forcing the Japanese to attack at a disadvantage. The Marines also discovered that in the jungle

▲ This 37mm Model 97 anti-tank gun was one of the few Japanese weapons that had an equivalent American counterpart. Although not a heavy weapon, it was not easily transportable in the jungle. (USMC 53480)

▶ A captured Japanese Model 92 mountain gun. This 70mm light field piece was used throughout the campaign by Japanese troops. It was one of the few pieces of artillery that could be broken down and manpacked. However, even when broken down it proved too much for the Japanese to carry over the terrain of Guadalcanal. The square box with leather handle contains the sight optics for the gun. The oblong metal box contains the tools and cleaning kit, and the upright metal box is the fixed ammunition container. (USMC 51015)

◀On Guadalcanal, Marines used a variety of weapons. In this picture, two types of the Reising .45-calibre submachine-gun are visible. The Marine in the left of the picture is holding the folding stock variant, while the Marine in the centre has the fixed stock. The Reising was not a preferred weapon and was prone to malfunctioning. The third Marine is cleaning a .30-calibre Browning Automatic Rifle (BAR), which was used as the squad automatic rifle and was a reliable, proven weapon. (USMC 51366)

flanking attacks on dug-in positions worked much better than frontal assaults.

American artillery was accurate and could deliver a high volume of high-angle fire either in the attack or on the defensive. The Japanese on the other hand launched most of their attacks unsupported, taking appalling losses. The M3A1 light tanks (Stuarts) brought ashore by the Marines were utilized effectively. They were light enough to be employed in the jungle clearings and superior to their Japanese counterparts.

Later, when the Army was brought in to reinforce and eventually to relieve the Marines, they also learned valuable lessons in jungle warfare. The fighting endured by the soldiers did not differ greatly from that of the Marines, but in most cases the equipment they carried and used was

◀ *Once ashore on Tulagi the Marines took over abandoned Japanese positions. Here a Marine 75mm Pak howitzer crew occupies a camouflaged Japanese gun position.*

The 75mm Pak was a light-weight infantry support weapon capable of being emplaced in confined spaces. (USMC 50515)

◀ *Sergeant Charles C. 'Monk' Arndt, dressed in the garb of a Japanese sniper, demonstrates how a sniper would ascend a palm tree on Guadalcanal. To assist his climb, Arndt uses Japanese climbing spikes which tie on to his field shoes and ease the climb. He is also wearing a woven fabric vest designed to blend the wearer into the tree top. Arndt was one of the three survivors of the ill-fated Goettge Patrol of 12-13 August. (USMC-50988)*

▼*M3A1 Stuart tanks of the 1st Tank Battalion on patrol, at Kukum Beach. These tanks operated primarily along the coastal plain and performed reconnaissance, screening and defensive roles. The Kukum area was the initial western boundary of the Marine perimeter. In the background are supply ships offloading at Lunga Point. (USMC 53256)*

Both the two piece fatigue suit of herringbone twill and the Marine inside it are starting to show the strain of the battle. Although of World War I vintage the M1918A2 Browning Automatic Rifle was still a reliable and popular weapon. (Shirley Mallinson)

newer and better. And when the Army arrived it came in force. Supply and communications problems were being solved, and the campaign was passing from a defensive into an offensive phase. By this time, the Americans had taken control of both sea and air lanes to the island.

(For purposes of clarifying Marine and Army unit regimental designators for the remainder of the text, Marine regiments are referred to as 'Marines' and Army regiments are referred to by branch. Thus the 1st Battalion, 5th Marine Regiment, is listed as the 1st Battalion, 5th Marines. The 1st Battalion, 164th Infantry Regiment, is listed as the 1st Battalion, 164th Infantry.)

The American Navy's entry to the campaign did not start off on a good note. The Battle of Savo Island was the worst naval disaster since Pearl Harbor. Most of the equipment on board the ships was First World War vintage. Radar was virtually new technology and was not effectively exploited.

The Navy learned its lessons in battle, and once an error was made it was seldom repeated. The naval battles fought for control of the waters surrounding Guadalcanal were violent in nature and occurred mostly during the hours of darkness. They were fought by ships ranging in size from PT boats up to battleships. The aircraft carrier, a mainstay for both sides, also played a decisive role in the campaign.

Damage control was another key aspect of the naval war. If a Japanese ship was damaged in a naval engagement it would have to be out of range of American aircraft from Guadalcanal by daylight – if not, it would be sunk by those planes. On the other hand, damaged American ships could be repaired at a series of 'local advanced naval bases' and be returned to fight again.

In the air the Americans had an advantage. Aircraft taking off from Guadalcanal could quickly engage the enemy and not use up tremendous quantities of fuel. Damaged aircraft could make emergency landings, and pilots could easily be rescued. The Grumman Wildcat fighter (F4F-4), was the mainstay Navy-Marine fighter for the campaign; although not as agile as the Zero it could out-dive it and absorb more punishment. And what the American pilots lacked in technology they made up for in skill and daring.

THE LANDINGS

Prior to the amhibious assault, very few people in the outside world had ever heard of Guadalcanal. Up to that point in time probably the only person who had mentioned it was Jack London in a turn of the century novel. The only information available was from planters and missionaries who had lived there in the past. Due to time constraints and fear that operational security would be compromised, there was no opportunity for intelligence patrols to conduct a reconnaissance. So, with somewhat sketchy information, the American forces departed for the objective area.

The Solomon Islands are a chain that extend from 163° E 12° S and run in a north-westerly direction to 153° E 5° S. They lie just below New Britain and New Ireland and are directly north and east of the tail of New Guinea. The larger islands of the group form two parallel chains separated by a long enclosed stretch of water that was later nicknamed the 'Slot'. Each of the longer islands, of which Guadalcanal is one, has a long axis that lies parallel to the chain as a whole. Several smaller islands and islets abound in the region: Florida, Tulagi, Gavutu and Tanambogo fall into these categories.

Because of their remoteness, there was not a great deal known about the Solomon Islands prior to the amphibious assault. What was known was not encouraging. Guadalcanal seemed a beautiful island from the air, but from the ground it would be difficult to conduct military operations. It is covered by a dense tropical rain forest that carpets the bulk of the island. Not far from the coastal area there are mountains, deep rivers, swamps, heat, humidity, rains and mud – all of which, when combined with the jungle, makes movement difficult. Here too was a breeding ground for various tropical diseases and fungi that would plague the soldiers of both sides.

The island itself is shaped like a rather large kidney bean, roughly sixty miles long by thirty miles wide. It has a large northern coastal plain, on which the Japanese had started their airfield. The coastal plain is covered by stretches of high, tough, razor-sharp kunai grass and is cut by many rivers that had no names or bridges across them. They generally ran from south to north stopping at the coast where their mouths were usually blocked by sand, forming stagnant pools. It was in this tropical wilderness, with its strange smells and animal sounds, that one of the major battles of the Pacific would take place.

▶ A posed picture taken on 7 August showing. General Vandegrift discussing invasion plans with his staff. Clockwise from the left are General Vandegrift, Commanding General; Lieutenant Colonel Thomas, Operations Officer; Lieutenant Colonel Pate, Logistics Officer; Lieutenant Colonel Goettge, Intelligence Officer; and Colonel James, Chief of Staff. (National Archives)

It was still dark (0400) on 7 August 1942 when the amphibious task force silently separated into two groups as it approached Savo Island. The Transport Division (TRANSDIV) was divided into two groups, X-RAY Guadalcanal and Y-OKE (Tulagi). The regiments of the 1st Marine Division consisted of two groups:

● The 5th Marines (Reinforced) less its 2nd Battalion, under the command of Colonel Leroy P. Hunt, was designated Combat Group A.

● Combat Group B was made up of the 1st Marines (Reinforced) under Colonel Clifton B. Cates.

These two combat groups, under Major General Alexander A. Vandegrift, the Division Commander, were to land on Guadalcanal, while smaller, more specialized groups of Y-OKE were organized to assault Florida, Tulagi, Gavutu and Tanambogo:

● The 1st Battalion, Second Marines, under Major Robert E. Hill, made up the Florida group.

● The Tulagi group was under Colonel Merritt A. Edson of the 1st Raider Battalion and included the 2nd Battalion, Fifth Marines, under Lieutenant Colonel Harold E. Rosecrans, and the 3rd Defense Battalion under Colonel Robert Pepper.

● The Gavutu and Tanambogo group were under Major Robert H. Williams of the 1st Parachute Battalion.

These smaller groups were under the command of Brigadier General William H. Rupertus, the Assistant Division Commander.

Both groups were task organized for the invasion: that is to say the 1st Marine Division had been reduced to a two-regiment division. The third regiment (7th Marines) had been detached for duty in British Samoa. (In reality, this was not the case and the division was actually far stronger than implied.) The 2nd Marines, who were normally part of the 2nd Marine Division, were added as were specialized units such as the 3rd Defense Battalion, the 1st Raider Battalion and the 1st Parachute Battalion. The division support group under Colonel Pedro A. Del Valle of the 11th Marines completed the force. A total of 1,959 officers and 18,146 enlisted Marines and Navy Corpsmen comprised the amphibious landing force on 7 August 1942.

Prior to their arrival in the area, the task force had conducted an amphibious rehearsal at Koro, in a remote portion of the Fiji Islands. The rehearsal, conducted in high surf conditions on beaches obstructed by coral reefs, was a disaster and was aborted to avoid injury to the personnel and damage to the precious landing craft. The planners who observed the rehearsal hoped that it would not be indicative of the upcoming landing!

The American amphibious forces were embarked on nineteen transports and four destroyer/transports. There were five cargo ships, eight cruisers, fourteen destroyers and five minesweepers. The accompanying carrier support group consisted of three carrier battle groups, *Saratoga*, *Enterprise* and *Wasp*. One battleship, *North Carolina*, and a force of cruisers and destroyers screened the battle groups. This force stayed to the south of Guadalcanal while the amphibious force sailed north, dividing in two when they approached Savo Island.

The movement to the amphibious objective area was shielded from the Japanese on Guadalcanal by one of the many tropical rain storms that frequent the region. Once the two groups separated they proceeded to their assigned beaches. After arriving on station, naval gunfire and carrier aircraft began to bombard their respective targets in accordance with the landing plan. The pattern of future campaigns in the Pacific was about to be demonstrated on the beaches of Tulagi and Guadalcanal.

Tulagi

The plan for the conquest of Tulagi was somewhat complicated. The Marine planners felt that in before Tulagi could be taken, certain key terrain features on nearby Florida Island would have to be captured.

At 0740 on 7 August 1942, 20 minutes before H-Hour, the first amphibious landing operation in the Solomon Islands was undertaken. It was made near the village of Haleta on Florida Island to secure a promontory that overlooked Beach Blue, the Tulagi invasion beach. The unit selected for the landing was reinforced Company B of the 1st Battalion, 2nd Marines, 2nd Marine Division, commanded by Captain Edgar J. Crane. The landing was unopposed and the western flank was secured quickly. An unopposed landing was also made by the remainder of the 1st Battalion, 2nd Marines, which landed at 0845 at Halavo on Florida Island to secure the eastern flank of the Gavutu landing.

Tulagi was attacked at 0800, according to schedule. The first to see action were the Marines of the 1st Raider Battalion, commanded by Colonel Merrit A. Edson, and they were followed by the 2nd Battalion, 5th Marines. As the landing craft approached Beach Blue, they ground to a halt on coral formations ranging from 30 to 100 yards out from the beach. The assault waves then began to make their way into the beach through water ranging from waist to armpit level. Upon reaching the shore, the Raiders and the 2nd Battalion, 5th Marines, began to make their way inland, the

▼The landing on Tulagi was made on the beach just south of the golf course by Marines of the 1st Raider Battalion, followed by the 2nd Battalion, 5th Marines. The Raiders then moved west and the 5th Marines moved east to capture the island. The date of the photograph (17.5.42) indicates it is an early intelligence photo and was undoubtedly one used to plan the assault. (USMC)

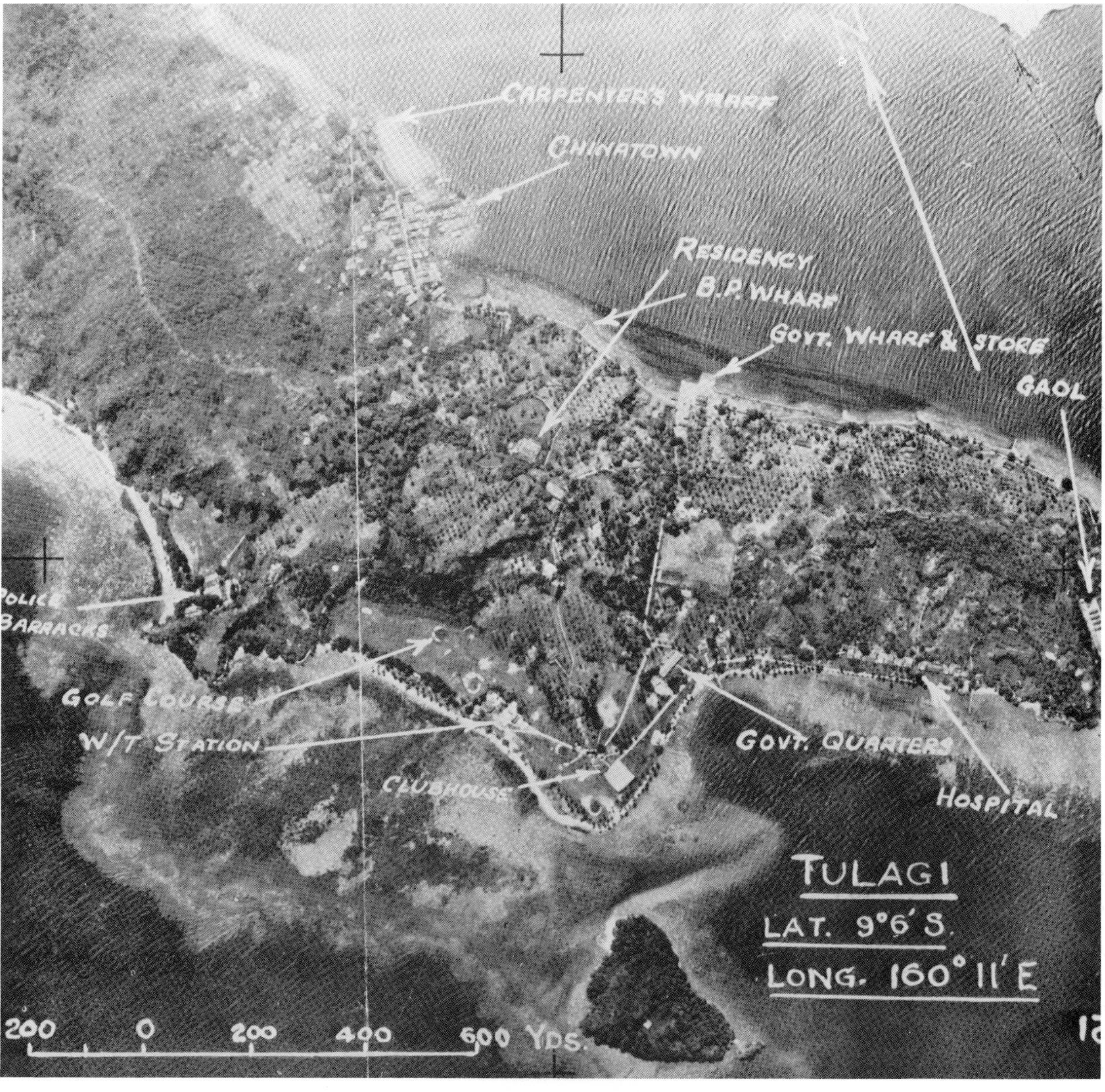

Raiders moving east and the 2nd Battalion, 5th Marines, moving north-west. Japanese resistance was encountered almost immediately by the Raiders but was systematically overcome. The advance continued slowly until dusk, when they consolidated and dug in for the night. This first night on Tulagi was to be indicative of many future nights in the Pacific: four separate attacks were launched by the Japanese to dislodge the Raiders

▶ *The advance west along Tulagi was made during the morning of 7 August by the Raiders. By 1120 they had advanced as far as Phase Line A. It took them the next day and a half to drive the remaining* *Japanese from the island. The fighting around Hill 280 with its cave complex was the most intense in the entire battle. (USMC)*

American Landing on Guadalcanal

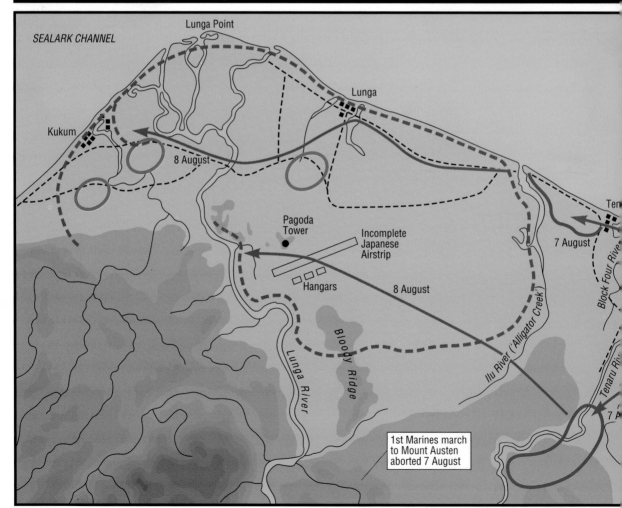

1st Marines march to Mount Austen aborted 7 August

American Landings on Florida, Tulagi, Tanambogo and Gavutu Islands

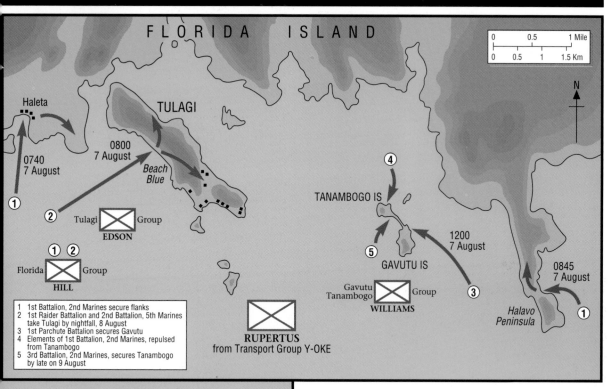

F L O R I D A   I S L A N D

0   0.5   1 Mile
0   0.5   1   1.5 Km

N

Haleta

TULAGI

0800
7 August

0740
7 August

Beach
Blue

① Tulagi ⨉ Group
② EDSON

TANAMBOGO IS

④

1200
7 August

⑤ GAVUTU IS

Florida ⨉ Group
① ② HILL

Gavutu
Tanambogo ⨉ Group
WILLIAMS

③

0845
7 August

Halavo
Peninsula

①

RUPERTUS
from Transport Group Y-OKE

1 1st Battalion, 2nd Marines secure flanks
2 1st Raider Battalion and 2nd Battalion, 5th Marines
   take Tulagi by nightfall, 8 August
3 1st Parchute Battalion secures Gavutu
4 Elements of 1st Battalion, 2nd Marines, repulsed
   from Tanambogo
5 3rd Battalion, 2nd Marines, secures Tanambogo
   by late on 9 August

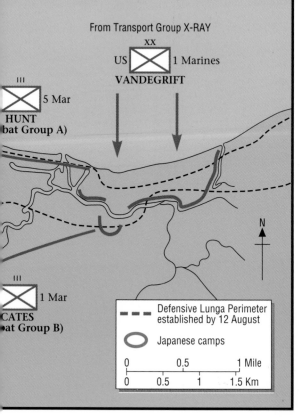

From Transport Group X-RAY

XX
US ⨉ 1 Marines
VANDEGRIFT

III
⨉ 5 Mar
HUNT
bat Group A)

III
⨉ 1 Mar
CATES
at Group B)

- - - Defensive Lunga Perimeter
      established by 12 August

◯ Japanese camps

0   0.5   1 Mile
0   0.5   1   1.5 Km

N

from their positions; each attack was beaten back.

The next day, the Marines resumed the offensive and encountered a stiff pocket of resistance in a deep man-made cut that ran north-south in the north-eastern portion of the island. The Japanese, taking advantage of the cut, dug positions into its base, from where they could bring fire to bear on the Raiders. Bringing up reinforcements, the Raiders isolated the enemy position on three sides; then, using improvised TNT-gasoline explosives, they systematically cleared this troublesome terrain feature and by the evening of the second day had eliminated effective Japanese resistance. For several days afterwards, isolated individuals and groups of Japanese continued to resist, but by nightfall on 8 August 1942, Tulagi was in Marine hands.

Gavutu and Tanambogo

These two small islets, each with prominent hills and connected by a causeway, were to be seized by two companies of the 1st Parachute Battalion led

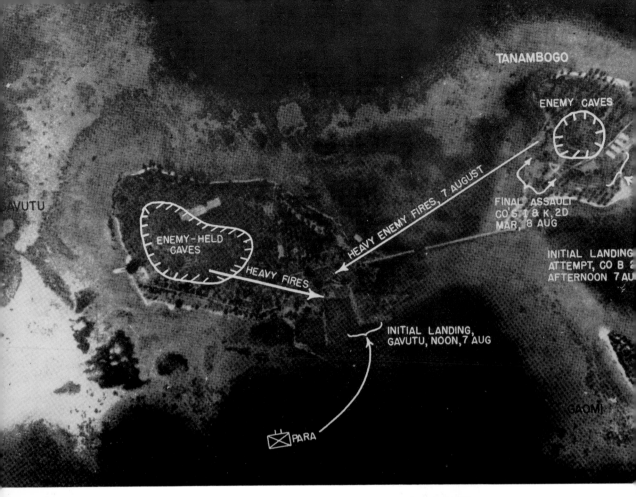

TANAMBOGO

ENEMY CAVES

GAVUTU

HEAVY ENEMY FIRES, 7 AUGUST

FINAL ASSAULT
CO'S I & K, 2D
MAR, 8 AUG

INITIAL LANDING
ATTEMPT, CO B 2
AFTERNOON 7 AU

ENEMY-HELD
CAVES

HEAVY FIRES

INITIAL LANDING,
GAVUTU, NOON, 7 AUG

GAOMI

PARA

▲The fighting on Gavutu and Tanambogo was fierce. This photograph shows the landing site of the Parachute Battalion and the locations from which they received heavy Japanese fire. Also shown are the landing sites of the companies from the 2nd Marine Division who attacked Tanambogo. (USMC)

◄Smoke rises from the gasoline supply dump on Tanambogo. It was struck by a shell from a naval gunfire ship supporting the landing on the night of 7 August. The photograph was taken the next day and shows the initial landing beach just to the right of the base of the column of smoke, and the final assault position located to the left and rear of the column. (USMC)

by Major Robert H. Williams. A third company would be held in reserve support for the assault companies. Gavutu, the higher in elevation of the two islands, was to be taken first.

The amphibious assault was to take place at H-Hour + 4 (1200) on 7 August. The plan called for a landing on the north-east coast. The naval gunfire support for the Gavutu amphibious assault was so effective, however, that it actually began to work against the Marines: so complete was the destruction that the original landing site, a concrete seaplane ramp, was reduced to rubble. The landing craft were forced to divert farther north to land the Parachutists and in so doing were exposed to flanking fire from Tanambogo. Despite heavy casualties, the Parachutists took the north-eastern portion of the island and its dominating hill, but to secure Gavutu, Tanambogo would have to be taken to stop its flanking fire, which was delaying the operation. Reinforcements were requested to undertake this phase of the operation.

Not being informed as to the number of reinforcements needed for Tanambogo, and with the bulk of his forces tied up on Tulagi, General Rupertus attached Company B, 1st Battalion, 2nd Marines, to the Parachutists. The Company reported to the Parachutists at 1800 and was informed that only a small Japanese force was on Tanambogo. It was felt that a night landing could be made and the Japanese quickly routed. The night amphibious assault was undertaken by Company B, minus one platoon, which did not take part as its landing craft had become stuck on the coral coming to Gavutu. The first boat came ashore without incident. As the second boat ground to a halt on the landing beach, a shell from a naval gunfire ship struck a nearby Japanese gasoline storage area, the explosion and resulting flare exposing the assaulting Marines. The ensuing battle was a nightmare. Unable to be reinforced, the attacking Marines were forced to withdraw under the most haphazardous conditions, the last making it back to Gavutu by 2200. Throughout the night, groups of Japanese counterattacked on Gavutu but were quickly repulsed.

On 8 August, the 3rd Battalion, 2nd Marines, was ordered to reinforce the parachutists on Gavutu and then attack Tanambogo. Supported by tanks from the 2nd Tank Battalion and with air and naval gunfire support, the 3rd Battalion, 2nd Marines made an amphibious landing at 1620 on 8 August 1942 on Tanambogo. Once a beachhead was established, reinforcements crossed the causeway, and by 2300, two-thirds of the island was secured. After a lot of fighting during the night, the island was completely secured by late on 9th.

Once Tanambogo fell, organized resistance in the Tulagi, Gavutu, Tanambogo and Florida Islands ceased. In all, the operation had taken three days. American losses overall were light, and the Japanese lost 1,500 troops. Only a handful of prisoners were taken.

Guadalcanal

On Guadalcanal an unopposed landing was made at Beach Red, about 6,000 yards east of Lunga Point. It was spearheaded by the 5th Marines, followed by the 1st Marines, and by 0930 the assault forces were ashore and moving inland. Their plan was simple: the 5th Marines would proceed along the coast, securing that flank, while the 1st Marines would move inland through the jungle and secure Mount Austen, described as a grassy knoll and reportedly only a short distance away. Now came the realization that intelligence concerning the terrain on Guadalcanal was faulty – Mount Austen was by no means a short way off, nor was it the grassy knoll as described. It was in fact the most prominent terrain feature in the area, more than four miles away and well outside the planned perimeter. It was not be captured until months later.

The remainder of the first day was spent consolidating positions and attempting to disperse the supplies that were stockpiling on the beach. Meanwhile the strongest Japanese countermeasure came at 1400 in the form of an air raid by eighteen twin-engined Type 97 bombers, two of which were shot down. A second wave of Type 99 Aichi bombers that came later was also repulsed with the loss of two aircraft; the cost to the Americans was a bomb hit on the destroyer *Mugford*.

At 2200, General Vandegrift issued the attack order for the next day. With Mount Austen out of

◀ Beach Red, which was about 6,000 yards east of Lunga Point, was the selected landing beach for Guadalcanal. Expecting to land under heavy fire, the Marines were relieved that the landing was unopposed. These Marines coming ashore are part of the initial waves. After crossing the beach, they moved inland to establish a beachhead. (National Achieves)

◀ The Japanese airfield on the morning of 7 August shows clearly how close the airfield was to completion. Hangers are seen in the left foreground, and the taxi way is clearly depicted. Smoke is billowing from a gasoline blaze set by off by fire from an American destroyer, seen to left of the column of smoke.

◀ Taxi-way to main runway is clearly defined, as are circular plane revetments. The structure to left is the pagoda type control tower that was set up by the Japanese to control airfield operations. The preparations made on the ground are clearly indicative of how far the Japanese had progressed to complete the airfield. (USMC)

This A6M2 of 6 Kokutai flew out of Rabaul during late 1942. During the Japanese counter attack of Guadalcanal, 'Operation I-GO', Zeros were staged from the main airfield at Rabaul to an advanced base at Buin on Bougainville. (Pilot Press copyright drawing)

reach and only 10,000 Marines ashore, he ordered the airfield to be taken and a defensive perimeter set up. The beachhead would be held temporarily to protect the off-loaded supplies until they could be moved into the perimeter. The next day, 8 August, therefore began with a westward advance by all Marine forces on Guadalcanal. The original objectives out of necessity had been changed, but the airfield remained the primary objective.

Contact with small groups of Japanese began to occur as the Marines closed on the airfield. In the Lunga region, just south of the airfield, defensive positions consisting of trenches and anti-aircraft emplacements, well built and equipped, were discovered deserted. The airfield, nearly 3,600 feet long and in its last stages of construction, was defended by a small group of Japanese who were attacked and killed. The hangers,

revetments and machine shops were all captured intact. Two large camps each with radio stations and other technical equipment were also captured.

By the end of the day, the airfield had been taken and a defensive perimeter established. As the Marines took over the Japanese camps in the area they came across large quantities of food, ammunition, weapons, trucks and other equipment

▼*After the assault troops had moved inland, Beach Red became somewhat chaotic. Not enough manpower was allocated to move the masses of supplies from the landing craft to the beach, and there was not enough motor transport to move supplies from the beach to the dumps. By the end of the first day the unloading of supplies had to be suspended, as there was no place on the beach to put them. The congestion depicted here is indicative of the problems experienced. (USMC 52193B)*

(some of which, unfortunately, was destroyed by improperly indoctrinated Marines). Except for some token resistance by Japanese stragglers, air action constituted the only major threat.

Originally it was thought that the Japanese were taken by surprise. Intelligence sources later revealed that the Japanese had been aware of the impending American assault but had thought it was only to be a raid. The Japanese higher command therefore had instructed the Japanese troops in the area to withdraw into the hills until the Americans departed.

A report from a Coastwatcher, Cecil J. Mason, on Bougainville, warned of a large group of Japanese aircraft heading toward Guadalcanal. This early warning message and many others that would follow from other Coastwatcher stations throughout the Solomon Islands would save many American lives throughout the campaign. (The Coastwatcher organization was started by Commander Eric Feldt of the Royal Australian Navy, the purpose being to report on Japanese activities in the Solomon Islands. The group was carefully recruited from local inhabitants of the area. The intelligence gathered by these individuals was passed back to the Coastwatcher HQ in Townesville, Australia, for processing and dissemination.) About an hour after Mason's message was received, forty twin-engined Japanese torpedo planes appeared, to find the amphibious task force alerted and manoeuvring at high speed.

So far the Japanese resistance had been less

▲The Coastwatchers were an organization set up by Lieutenant Commander Eric Feldt (middle row, second from left). Their mission was to gather intelligence in the Solomon Islands and forward it on via radio communications to the Townesville, Australia, headquarters.

than effective. In the air, attacks were repulsed with minimum damage to the Americans. However, the Japanese had no intention of giving up the Solomon Islands without a fight.

◄As the Marines moved through the Lunga area south of the airfield they captured vast stocks of Japanese equipment and foodstuffs. This particular building, which housed a vast quantity of rice, was captured in the first few days. Note the palm frond camouflage hastily applied to the roof by the Japanese. (USMC 53436)

▼ *Some captured buildings were immediately converted for effective use. This particular one houses the 1st Marine Division switchboard and has been named the Guadalcanal Telephone and Telegraph. The smaller sign over the door says USO Club and was typical of Marine humour throughout the campaign. (USMC 61556)*

▲ *The Japanese ice plant, which was initially vandalized by Marines and later repaired. The plant was the only steady source of ice for the Marines throughout the campaign. Luxuries such as this were few and far between on Guadalcanal and demonstrated the primitive conditions encountered. (USMC 50493)*

Japanese captured on Guadalcanal were a valuable source of information for the Marines. Once captured, prisoners were usually cooperative. In this picture, a daily roll call is taken. The Japanese soldier to the right of the Marine in the picture is the translator. (USMC-51430)

AUGUST

Early on 8 August, part of the Japanese 8th Fleet under Admiral Mikawa made preparations to strike at the American amphibious task force. Mikawa's battle group consisted of five heavy cruisers and two light cruisers plus a destroyer. With this formidable force he began to move south. En route, he was spotted by an Allied patrol plane and there began a tragic chain of events that would lead to one of the greatest naval disasters ever suffered by the American Navy.

The Battle of Savo Island

Perceiving that he had been spotted, Mikawa reversed course until the plane had left the area; then he came back to his original course. The spotter pilot did not report the sighting until after returning to his base – and then only after having tea. The message was then sent to Australia in code and then decoded; it was then encoded and sent to the American Navy at Guadalcanal. When it arrived at its destination at 1800, there was some confusion about which direction the Japanese were heading.

After receiving the warning about the approaching Japanese, Admiral Turner positioned two destroyers, *Blue* and *Ralph Talbot*, north-west of Savo Island, to maintain a radar watch on the channel. He then positioned three cruisers, the *Australia*, *Canberra* and *Chicago*, along with two destroyers, the *Bagley* and *Patterson* to patrol between Savo Island and Cape Esperance. Three additional cruisers, *Vincennes*, *Astoria* and *Quincy*, along with two destroyers, *Helm* and *Jarvis*, were to patrol between Savo Island and Florida Island. Two other cruisers and two destroyers guarded the transports.

As these events were occurring, Admiral Fletcher, in command of the carrier support group, felt that operational losses to his aircraft and dwindling fuel oil for his ships limited his effectiveness. Predicated on this, he asked Admiral Ghormley for permission to retire from the area. Permission was granted and Fletcher announced that the aircraft carriers would be withdrawn from the area on 9 August. Once Admiral Turner was aware of Fletcher's plans he called General Vandegrift and Admiral Crutchley to his flagship, the latter arriving on one of his cruisers, thus removing a major warship from the protective screen at a critical time. Turner informed his officers that once Fletcher retired from the area he would not be able to remain. Vandegrift argued that over half his supplies were still on the transports. Turner informed him that with the absence of air cover

◀ *This early view of Henderson Field shows that the Japanese had nearly completed its construction. Only the north-west corner of the runway remains to be* *levelled and surfaced. Note that the trees in the coconut plantation to the right have been cut down to make room for the airfield. (National Archives)*

▶One of General Vandegrift's primary concerns was the threat of a Japanese seaborne invasion, so the bulk of the Division's assets were set up to repel a counter-landing. This M3A1 light tank is dug in and camouflaged as part of a beach defensive position. (USMC 50934)

he would withdraw the transports the next morning.

General Vandegrift complained bitterly. The withdrawal of the amphibious task force at a time as critical as this could have disastrous effects. The landing plan was predicated on amphibious shipping to remain in the area until 11 August 1942. This was set up in order to off-load the supplies essential for successful prosecution of the campaign ashore. Turner understood – but his decision would remain unchanged. And, at 1810 on 8 August, Fletcher began to withdraw his carriers.

Meanwhile, the Japanese cruisers were approaching Savo Island undetected. Shortly before arriving there, they launched float planes, which flew over the American and Australian ships. The ships did not fire as they assumed the float planes were American since they were flying with their recognition lights on. About 0145 on 9 August, the planes began to drop flares illuminating the American ships. At the same time, the Japanese naval force miraculously slipped past the radar picket destroyers.

In the ensuing night naval engagement, which developed into a wild mêlée, the Japanese scored a major victory. In what is now referred to as the Battle of Savo Island, the Allies lost four cruisers, with one cruiser and one destroyer damaged. The Japanese sustained damage to only one of their destroyers.

The Battle of Savo Island was one of the worst defeats ever suffered by the American Navy. The Japanese had achieved the element of surprise and defeated the American force in detail. *Vincennes* and *Quincy* were sunk within the first hour of the attack. *Canberra* was hit badly; she burned all night and was sunk the next day by American destroyers to prevent possible capture, while *Astoria* sank at about 1130 on the 9th. *Chicago* and the destroyer *Ralph Talbot* were badly damaged.

Fortunately, Admiral Mikawa did not attack the transport area. Had he done so he could have effectively curtailed American operations in the area. Instead he broke contact and headed back to Rabaul to be out of range of American carrier aircraft. Meanwhile, the damage inflicted by the Japanese on the amphibious task force delayed its departure until 1200 on 9 August. By 1500, the first group of ships had departed; the last group left at 1830.

The First Week

With the withdrawal of the amphibious task force the Marines were left without air support. They began to take stock of their perimeter and inventoried their captured supplies. The withdrawal of the transports had left the Marines with only part of their supplies: ammunition was adequate, but food was a much more serious issue. Even with the acquisition of a considerable quantity of Japanese foodstuffs, supplies were so short that on 12 August the division went on a two meal a day programme.

The captured airfield, which had nearly been completed by its former occupants, was renamed Henderson Field in honour of Major Lofton E. Henderson, a Marine pilot killed at the Battle of Midway.

It was realized early on that for the Guadalcanal operation to have a successful outcome,

◀ *On the morning of 9 August, General Vandegrift called his principal staff officers to his command post, which was located near a small ridge east of the Lunga River. Vandegrift informed them of the losses sustained by the American Navy at the Battle of Savo Island and of the subsequent withdrawal of the amphibious shipping. Shortly after the meeting adjourned the officers were asked to pose for this photograph. Vandegrift, fourth from left, is seated among the officers who would not only lead the division to victory on Guadalcanal but through the entire Pacific war. (USMC 50509)*

◀ *Patrols such as this one were sent out to gather intelligence on the Japanese. In the early days of the campaign, these patrols proved invaluable. Patrols travelled light but were usually heavily armed. This particular patrol carries a variety of weapons: M1903 Springfield rifles, M-1 Garands and BARs. They have captured a Japanese soldier who will hopefully provide intelligence on Japanese forces in the area. (USMC 58860)*

Henderson Field would have to be developed. Until it was completed, the Marines would be at the mercy of any air or naval attacks the Japanese cared to launch. A survey of the field conducted on the day of its capture indicated that 2,600 feet of runway could be finished in two days and that the remaining stretch of 1,178 feet could be completed in a week. The task could have been completed much faster, but the engineers had virtually no earth moving equipment. Fortunately there was some Japanese equipment available, and it was quickly pressed into service.

It would not be until 20 August that the Marines would have aircraft based on the island. On that day, nineteen planes of VMF-223 (F4F–4s under Major John L. Smith) and twelve dive-bombers of VMSB 232 (SBD–3s under Lieutenant Colonel Richard C. Mangrum) would land, their first mission being to assist at the Battle of the Tenaru. The Marine planes would be followed on 22 and 27 August by elements of the Army Air Corps 667 Fighter Squadron with 14 P-400s. The P-400 was an export version of the P-39, and was a Lend-Lease aircraft that did not have adapters for the American oxygen system, which necessitated their use in a ground support role. (The standard joke at the time was that a P-400 was a P-40 with a Zero on its tail.)

In the first week the tone of the campaign was set. Daily – and this was to continue for months – except when weather and American fighter aircraft were present, Japanese planes made incessant air raids. The targets were either Henderson Field or resupply shipping at Lunga Point. At night the perimeter was bombarded by Japanese warships offshore or by submarines (nicknamed 'Oscar'), which were more a nuisance than anything else. Two other characters that fell into this latter category were: 'Louie the Louse', a Japanese plane that periodically flew over dropping flares, which usually preceded a naval bombardment; and, 'Washing Machine Charlie', a Japanese plane with its engines set deliberately out of synchronization, the mission of which was more harassment than bombing.

All in all, the situation looked pretty bleak for the Marines, virtually abandoned by the Navy and left to fend for themselves on a remote tropical island. With the lack of adequate supplies and equipment, necessity became the mother of invention. They adapted to their new jungle home and began to carve out some creature comforts.

Having quickly established themselves ashore, they began to improve the perimeter. Considering a Japanese invasion more than likely, General Vandegrift concentrated the bulk of his combat units along the beach. A defensive line was dug along the beach running east from 'Alligator Creek', where the eastern flank was denied to the south, giving the defending Marines holding the river line a tactical advantage. To the west the line ran to Kukum, and then the flank was refused south towards a low range of jungle hills. The southern sector was initially dismissed as an avenue of approach for the Japanese, as it was almost impenetrable. This line was held by support troops manning a series of outposts on the grassy hills that dotted the region.

Once the Lunga Perimeter was established, patrols were sent out to gain information on the Japanese forces on the island. So far as could be determined, the bulk of the Japanese forces were concentrated west of the perimeter, in the Matanikau River and Point Cruz area. To verify this information it was decided to send out two patrols on 12 August 1942: one would head east to Tetere, and one would reconnoitre west past the Matanikau.

The Goettge Patrol

The western patrol, commanded by the Division Intelligence Officer, Colonel Frank B. Goettge, departed with 23 Marines, one Navy surgeon and a Japanese prisoner. Originally intended as a reconnaissance mission, the patrol was to depart during the day. It was scheduled to land west of Point Cruz and to conduct a reconnaissance of the western Matanikau region, move into the hills to the south and bivouac overnight. Next day it would move eastwards and return to the Marine perimeter. Once Goettge assumed command of the patrol, however, certain outside influences began to cause changes in its composition. A Japanese prisoner, a naval warrant officer, had disclosed under repeated questioning that some of his

▲ *Colonel Frank B. Goettge, the Division intelligence officer who led the ill-fated patrol that landed near the Matanikau River on 12-13 August. The patrol* *encountered strong Japanese resistance and was overwhelmed. Only three Marines escaped to give an account of the fight. (Author's Collection)*

comrades in the Matanikau region might be induced to surrender. The fact that he was notably reticent and did not volunteer the information contributed to his credibility. Also, some Marines who had turned a Japanese triple barrelled pom-pom gun in the direction of the Matanikau and fired off some rounds reported a white surrender flag. The flag probably was an ordinary Japanese flag with the red centre not visible to the observers. Based on this sketchy information, Goettge persuaded General Vandegrift to allow him to lead a patrol down to the Matanikau region possibly to accept the surrender of the Japanese.

Believing in the possibility of a Japanese surrender Goettge changed the primary patrol mission from reconnaissance to 'humanitarian'. These additional details caused a considerable delay, and the patrol did not depart until dusk. It left from Kukum beach on 12 August and either by intention or by accident, landed east instead of west of Point Cruz, near the Matanikau River.

Shortly after landing, Goettge and a few selected Marines made a quick reconnaissance. As they approached Matanikau village, they ran into a small Japanese force. Goettge was killed, and one Marine was wounded. The Marines pulled back to the beach to join the main body of the patrol. Had they all moved south or west at that moment, they would have undoubtedly survived. However, it was decided to form a defensive position at the water's edge and signal for assistance.

In a battle that raged through the night, the small patrol fought an even increasing number of Japanese. Two Marines, Sergeant Charles C. 'Monk' Arndt and Corporal Joseph Spaulding, were sent out at different intervals to bring help. Despite heroic efforts on their part, the terrain and Japanese forces in the area slowed their travel time to the Marine Perimeter, and by the time they got back and made their reports it was too late to save the beleaguered Marines. The patrol, which fought on through the night, was finally overwhelmed at dawn. The lone survivor, Sergeant Frank L. Few, stated he had observed the Japanese mutilating the dead as he swam away from the battle area.

A relief force was sent out the next morning and landed west of Point Cruz, the patrol's original destination, but could find no trace of it or a battle.

This, of course, started a rumour that the clever Japanese had killed the patrol and obliterated any trace of the battle. In reality, the rescuing Marines who were not familiar with the area, had landed at the wrong location and had bypassed the battle area as they returned to the perimeter.

The loss of the patrol overshadowed the good news that Henderson Field was declared operational. The first plane to land was a Navy PBY-5A Catalina, which evacuated two Marines, a method that was to be used throughout the campaign.

The Brush Patrol

The progress of the patrol sent east was less eventful. As it moved through a native village it came across a Catholic priest, who advised them that the Japanese had landed a force to the east near Koli Point; two days later, on 14 August, this information was verified by a Coastwatcher, W. F.

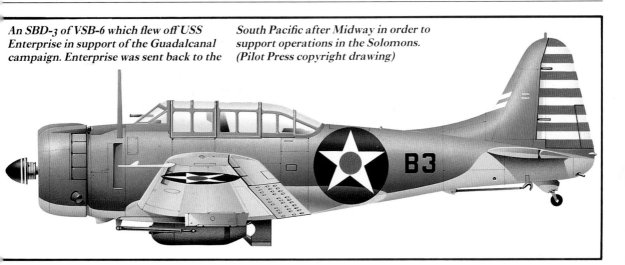

An SBD-3 of VSB-6 which flew off USS Enterprise in support of the Guadalcanal campaign. Enterprise was sent back to the South Pacific after Midway in order to support operations in the Solomons. (Pilot Press copyright drawing)

Martin Clemens, a District Officer assigned to Guadalcanal and a Captain in the British Protectorate Defence Force Solomon Islands Civil Government who had been hiding up in the hills from the Japanese. He had been instrumental in keeping information on Japanese activity flowing back to Australia prior to the Americans coming ashore. As soon as he was convinced that the Americans were going to stay, he came down from his hiding place and rendered valuable assistance. Making full use of his knowledge of Guadalcanal and its natives, he established an intelligence network of native scouts that proved invaluable during the campaign.

To verify the strength of the Japanese in the region, another patrol was sent out on 19 August. This patrol was led by Captain Charles C. Brush, and although its primary mission was reconnaissance, it had sufficient combat power to take care of itself. As it made its way toward Koli Point it stumbled into a large party of Japanese. In the ensuing fire-fight, 31 Japanese were killed.

▶ *Captain Martin Clemens and some of his Solomon Islander scouts. Clemens had been a district officer with the British Government before the war. After entering the American lines, Clemens helped organize a scouting force made up of local natives that provided a valuable source of accurate information throughout the campaign. (USMC 50505)*

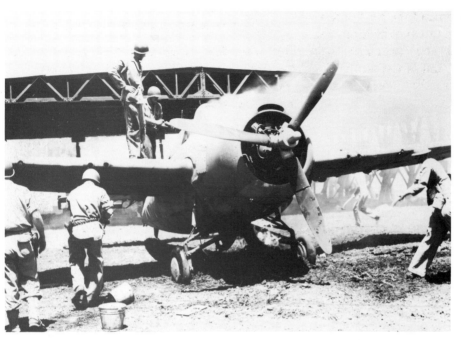

◀ The Grumman F4F-4 (Wildcat) was the first type of aircraft to be based at Henderson Field. It was a sturdy, dependable aircraft capable of sustained operations in punishing conditions. This particular plane is an early variant and has the heavy propeller. Note the propeller itself is bullet scarred, indicating that the aircraft has seen combat. This aircraft was saved to fight again by the quick-thinking Marines who extinguished the flames when it was set afire during one of the daily bombing raids. (USMC 50516)

◀ The SBD Douglas (Dauntless) dive-bomber was another mainstay aircraft used by the Marines on Guadalcanal. Normally it carried a crew of two, pilot and rear gunner, and could drop a 500-pound bomb from a mount under the fuselage. It was also capable of carrying two 250-pound bombs mounted on bomb racks located under each wing. (USMC 55786)

◀ These P-400s were used by the Army 67th Fighter Squadron. It was an export version of the P-39 and could not be fitted with oxygen bottles, so it had a 12,000 feet ceiling. It was used in a ground support role. Its 120mm nose cannon, two .50-calibre and four .30-calibre machine-guns, coupled with the ability to carry a 500-pound bomb, made this plane an extremely effective close support weapon. (USMC 50467)

The uniforms and insignia of the dead Japanese indicated that this was a group of high ranking officers and senior enlisted men. Apparently they were on a reconnaissance mission to verify the Marine lines in preparation for a concentrated attack from the east.

The First Battle of the Matanikau

That same day, the 19th, on the western side of the perimeter a battalion sized operation was being launched against the Japanese in the Matanikau area, its mission being to drive the Japanese out of

▶ *The steep banks and jungle terrain are evident in this ground level view of the Matanikau River. This peaceful looking river was made almost impossible to cross by the Japanese troops who tenaciously defended its western banks. (USMC 59649)*

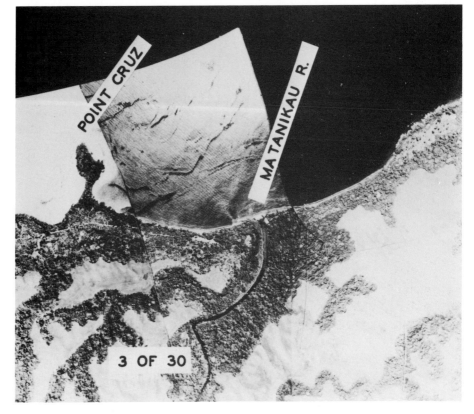

▶ *The Matanikau region was the most hotly contested area of the entire Guadalcanal campaign. The river, which had steep banks, cut through a deep valley and gave the Japanese, who were usually concentrated between it and Point Cruz, an excellent defensive line. This aerial photograph provides an excellent overall perspective of the region. (USMC)*

POINT CRUZ

MATANIKAU R.

3 OF 30

August-September 1942 Operations on Guadalcanal

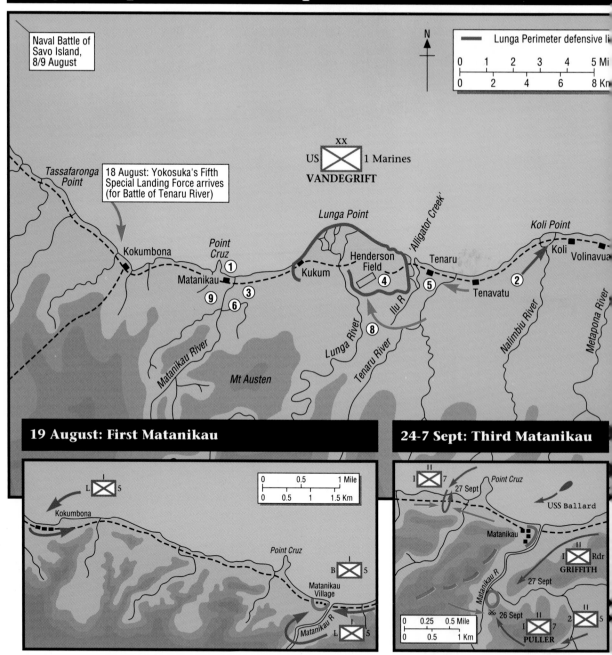

Naval Battle of Savo Island, 8/9 August

Lunga Perimeter defensive li

0 1 2 3 4 5 Mi
0 2 4 6 8 Km

Tassafaronga Point

18 August: Yokosuka's Fifth Special Landing Force arrives (for Battle of Tenaru River)

US VANDEGRIFT XX 1 Marines

Lunga Point

Koli Point

Kokumbona

Point Cruz ①

Henderson Field ④

Tenaru ⑤ Koli Volinavua

Matanikau ③ ⑨ ⑥

Kukum

② Tenavatu

Alligator Creek

Ilu R.

Nalimbiu River

Metapona River

Lunga River

Tenaru River

⑧

Matanikau River

Mt Austen

19 August: First Matanikau

L ⊠ 5

0 0.5 1 Mile
0 0.5 1 1.5 Km

Kokumbona

Point Cruz

B ⊠ 5

Matanikau Village

Matanikau R.

L ⊠ 5

24-7 Sept: Third Matanikau

I ⊠ 7

27 Sept

Point Cruz

USS Ballard

Matanikau

I ⊠ Rdr GRIFFITH

27 Sept

Matanikau R.

26 Sept

0 0.25 0.5 Mile
0 0.5 1 Km

I ⊠ 7 PULLER 2 ⊠ 5

the region. One Company (Company B, 1st Battalion, 5th Marines) was to approach using the coastal road and fight a spoiling action at the river mouth, while a second company (Company L, 3rd Battalion, 5th Marines) was to move overland through the jungle and deliver the main attack from the south. The third company (Company I, 3rd Battalion, 5th Marines) would make a seaborne landing to the west near Kokumbona village and cut off any retreating Japanese.

In what would be called the First Battle of the Matanikau, the Marines conducted an attack that succeeded in destroying the small Japanese garrison in the area. During the consolidation phase

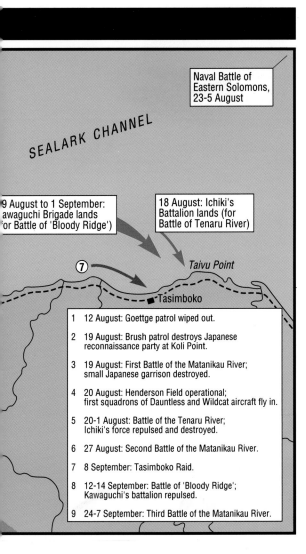

Naval Battle of
Eastern Solomons,
23-5 August

SEALARK CHANNEL

9 August to 1 September:
Kawaguchi Brigade lands
for Battle of 'Bloody Ridge')

18 August: Ichiki's
Battalion lands (for
Battle of Tenaru River)

⑦

Taivu Point

Tasimboko

1	12 August: Goettge patrol wiped out.
2	19 August: Brush patrol destroys Japanese reconnaissance party at Koli Point.
3	19 August: First Battle of the Matanikau River; small Japanese garrison destroyed.
4	20 August: Henderson Field operational; first squadrons of Dauntless and Wildcat aircraft fly in.
5	20-1 August: Battle of the Tenaru River; Ichiki's force repulsed and destroyed.
6	27 August: Second Battle of the Matanikau River.
7	8 September: Tasimboko Raid.
8	12-14 September: Battle of 'Bloody Ridge'; Kawaguchi's battalion repulsed.
9	24-7 September: Third Battle of the Matanikau River.

of the action, the mutilated remains of the Marines of Colonel Goettge's patrol were discovered, thus clearing up the 'mystery' of the missing patrol.

The Battle of the Tenaru

On 13 August, the Japanese High Command ordered Lieutenant General Haruyoshi Hyakutake's Seventeenth Army at Rabaul to retake Guadalcanal. The naval commander for this operation was to be Rear Admiral Raizo Tanaka. With no clear intelligence picture of the American forces on Guadalcanal, Hyakutake decided to retake it with 6,000 troops from the 7th Division's 28th Infantry Regiment and the Yokosuka Special

Naval Landing Force. These units would be followed by the 35th Brigade.

The spearpoint of the effort would be made by the reinforced 2nd Battalion of the 28th Infantry Regiment, led by Colonel Kiyono Ichiki. Ichiki and an advance element of 900 of his troops were taken to Guadalcanal and landed at Taivu Point on the night of 18 August 1942. At the same time 500 troops of the Yokosuka Fifth Special Landing Force went ashore to the west at Kokumbona.

These landings were the first run of what would be nicknamed the 'Tokyo Express' by the Marines. It was basically a shuttle run organized by Admiral Tanaka. Composed of cruisers, destroyers and transports, it shuttled troops and supplies at night from Rabaul to Guadalcanal. The route they took down the Solomons chain was nicknamed the 'Slot'.

After landing at Taivu, Colonel Ichiki established his headquarters, sent out scouting parties and awaited the arrival of the remainder of his regiment. Once he had the rest of his troops and accurate intelligence on the Americans he would attack. The intelligence picture Ichiki had was that a raiding party of Americans was cowering in a defensive perimeter around the airfield. Ichiki's plan was to march to the former Japanese construction camp east of the Tenaru, establish it as his headquarters and then move against the Americans. After learning that his scouting party had been destroyed by the Marine patrol on 19 August, Ichiki changed his plans. Fearing he had lost the element of surprise he decided to march westwards with the troops he had to hand. His knowledge of the terrain east of the Tenaru was incomplete, but he did not expect to encounter any Americans east of the airfield.

On the night of 20/21 August, Marine listening posts on the east bank of Alligator Creek, (then believed to be the Tenaru River) detected the movement of a large body of Japanese troops. The listening posts had no sooner withdrawn than a severely wounded native, Jacob Vouza, a sergeant in the native police contingent, stumbled into the Marine lines and, before collapsing, imparted the news that the Japanese were going to attack. Vouza had been captured, tortured and bayoneted by the Japanese in an attempt to gain information on the

▲*Colonel Kiyono Ichiki was the leader of the 900-man Japanese force that attacked the Marines at 'Alligator Creek'. Contrary to popular belief, he did not commit suicide after burning his regimental colours after the aborted attack: last seen he was rallying his men as they attacked the Marines. More than likely he was killed attempting to cross the sand spit. (USMC)*

▲*Sergeant Jacob Vouza of the Solomon Islands police force was on his way to his village at Roroni when he was captured by the Japanese. After finding an American flag on Vouza, the Japanese tortured him to obtain information on the Americans. Bayoneted and left for dead, Vouza managed to make it to the Marine lines to warn them of Ichiki's impending attack. (USMC)*

Americans. Left for dead, he had managed to make his way to the Marine lines. (Honoured by the Allies for his heroism, Vonza was later knighted and died in 1984 at the age of 92; his statue is the centrepiece of a memorial unveiled on 7 August 1992 on Guadalcanal.)

No sooner had Vouza arrived than the first Japanese, who were marching in formation, ran into a single strand of barbed wire placed across the sand bar at the mouth of the creek. This temporarily disorganized the leading elements of Ichiki's force, who were not expecting to run into any defensive positions so far east.

The ensuing battle that erupted, which would later be referred to erroneously as the Battle of the Tenaru, was fierce and savage. Using human wave tactics, the Japanese attempted to crush Lieutenant Colonel Edwin A. Pollock's 2nd Battalion, 1st Marines, which was defending the area.

Unable to dislodge the Marines, who were now using heavy machine-gun fire and canister fire from two 37mm anti-tank weapons to decimate his troops, Ichiki sent part of his force south along the east bank to cross the creek upstream in an attempt to outflank the Marines. This attempt failed. He then sent a company out through the surf in an attempt to break through from the north. This attempt also failed. The last anyone saw of Colonel Ichiki he was moving forward towards the sand bar, where he was undoubtedly killed.

Mount Austen   Henderson Field

Ilu River

▲This picture shows the east bank of 'Alligator Creek' (referred to as the Ilu River). Ichiki launched his attack from the east across the sand bar. The Marines occupied the west bank and stopped Ichiki's attack. Henderson Field, Ichiki's objective, is seen in the background. (US Navy)

►This is the sand bar at the mouth of 'Alligator Creek' where Colonel Ichiki attempted to cross. In the confusion of the battle, the creek was misidentified as the Tenaru River, and the battle fought there has always borne the name 'Battle of the Tenaru'. This position is from the Marine side looking east towards the direction of the Japanese attack. (USMC 54891)

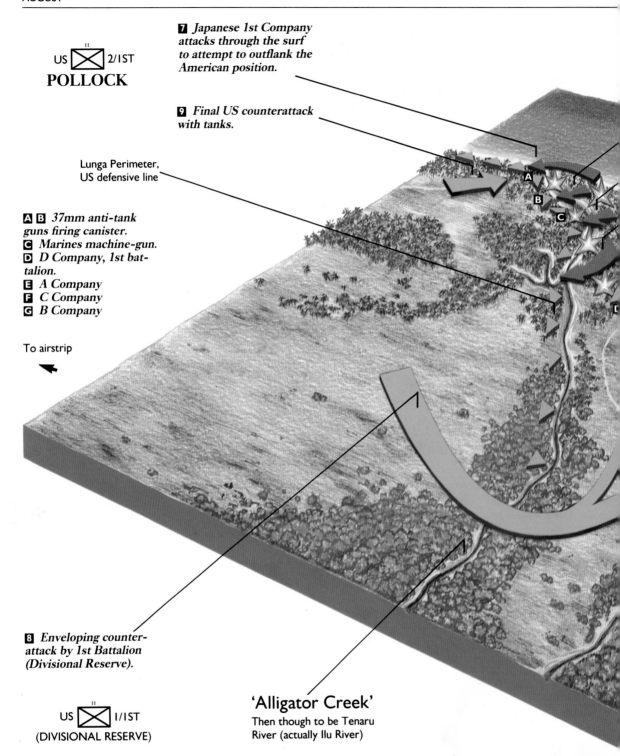

US ⊠ 2/IST
POLLOCK

7 *Japanese 1st Company attacks through the surf to attempt to outflank the American position.*

9 *Final US counterattack with tanks.*

Lunga Perimeter,
US defensive line

A B *37mm anti-tank guns firing canister.*
C *Marines machine-gun.*
D *D Company, 1st battalion.*
E *A Company*
F *C Company*
G *B Company*

To airstrip

8 *Enveloping counter-attack by 1st Battalion (Divisional Reserve).*

US ⊠ I/IST
(DIVISIONAL RESERVE)

'Alligator Creek'
Then though to be Tenaru
River (actually Ilu River)

BATTLE OF THE TENARU

20–21 August 1942

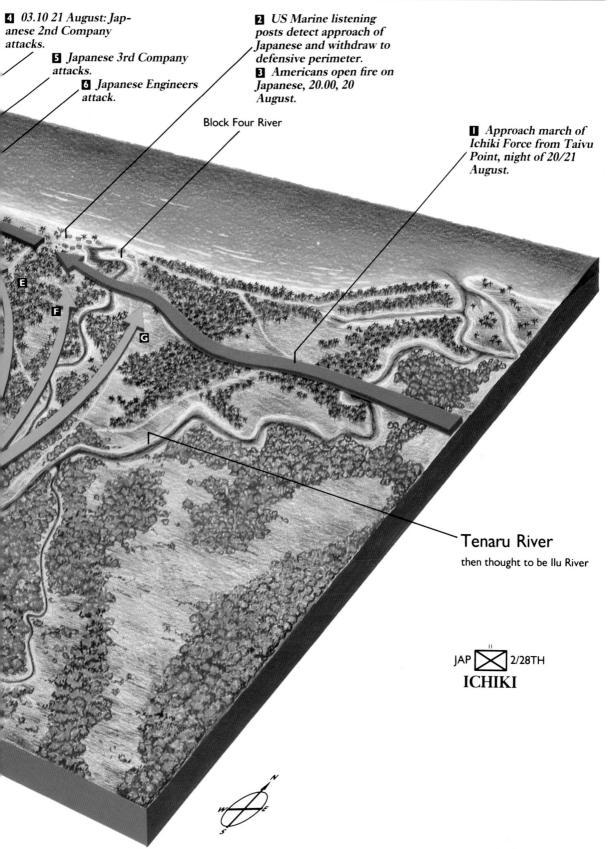

4 *03.10 21 August: Japanese 2nd Company attacks.*

5 *Japanese 3rd Company attacks.*

6 *Japanese Engineers attack.*

2 *US Marine listening posts detect approach of Japanese and withdraw to defensive perimeter.*

3 *Americans open fire on Japanese, 20.00, 20 August.*

Block Four River

1 *Approach march of Ichiki Force from Taivu Point, night of 20/21 August.*

E

F

G

Tenaru River

then thought to be Ilu River

JAP 2/28TH

ICHIKI

N

W E

S

◀ This Marine tank and its crew were part of the enveloping force that destroyed Ichiki's troops after crossing over the creek at its mouth. The canister fire from the 37mm cannon and the machine-gun fire from the tanks' 30-calibre light machine-guns wreaked havoc on the Japanese. (USMC 50560)

◀ The aftermath of the Battle of the Tenaru clearly indicates the determination of the Japanese attackers. The dead Japanese in the foreground had actually penetrated to the west bank of the creek before they were stopped by the defending Marines. The Marines in the background are walking through the area to survey the aftermath of the battle. (National Archives 80-G-M077

◀ Japanese soldiers of the Ichiki detachment lie dead on the beach after they were shot trying to outflank the Marines. This group moved through the surf and attempted to attack from the north. (USMC)

The fight continued throughout the night. In the battle, one machine-gun team distinguished itself by its overt acts of bravery. The weapon was deployed near the mouth of the river and was exacting a heavy toll on the Japanese attackers. In an attempt to silence the gun, the Japanese killed the gunner, Private Johnny Rivers, but not before his finger froze on the trigger and 200 more rounds were fired. Private Albert Schmid took over the gun; and Corporal Leroy Diamond helped him spot targets until he was wounded. Schmid continued to fire at the Japanese until a grenade landed in front of him. The resulting explosion and fragmentation blinded Schmid; however, he attempted to continue fighting the Japanese. For their action, both Schmid and Diamond would receive the Navy Cross, the Navy-Marine Corps' second highest award for bravery.

In the morning the Marines were still holding. It was then decided to conduct a double envelopment to eliminate Ichiki's force. Supported by light tanks, artillery and newly arrived fighter planes, the 1st Battalion, 1st Marine Regiment, which had been held as Division reserve, outflanked Ichiki's force and destroyed it. Of the original 900 Japanese troops, 800 were dead or dying on the sand bar and in the surrounding jungle. The cost to the Marines was light: 34 killed and 75 wounded.

This bridge, constructed after the Battle of the Tenaru, gives an indication of the terrain the Marines who enveloped Ichiki had to move through. It was undoubtedly terrain like this that caused Ichiki to launch his attack over the sand bar rather than attempt a flanking movement. (USMC 50465)

The Battle of the Eastern Solomons

While the issue on land was being decided the Japanese assembled a major naval task force under Admirals Tanaka and Mikawa. At the same time an American naval task force under Admiral Fletcher which was operating south-east of the lower Solomons in what it believed to be a safe area, became engaged in the Battle of the Eastern Solomons.

Unaware of what had happened to Ichiki, the Japanese had planned on reinforcing him with a larger secondary force of about 1,500 troops. This force departed on 19 August in four transports screened by four destroyers. They were to land on Guadalcanal on 24 August. To support the transports and operations ashore the Japanese dispatched two naval task forces composed of five aircraft carriers, four battleships, sixteen cruisers and thirty destroyers.

Three American carrier groups, comprising three aircraft carriers, one battleship, six cruisers and eighteen destroyers, were operating about a hundred miles south-east of Guadalcanal. Somehow, an erroneous intelligence report on 23 August indicated that the large Japanese force, believed to be in the area, was returning to the Japanese base at Truk Island. Operating on this mistaken belief, one of the carrier groups centred around *Wasp* departed from the group to refuel.

This left two carrier groups formed around *Enterprise* and *Saratoga*. Shortly after the *Wasp* group departed, patrol planes discovered the Japanese transport group 350 miles from Guadalcanal. The next day, 24 August, American carrier planes discovered the Japanese forces, and at the same time Japanese carrier planes discovered the American forces.

In the ensuing air-to-ship, air-to-air battle, the smaller American force turned back a larger Japanese force. The Japanese were able to land 1,500 troops and bombard Henderson Field; but they were not able to intervene in the ground fighting. Also, they were no longer able to control the air space over Guadalcanal. The Japanese lost the carrier *Ryujo*, one destroyer, one light cruiser and ninety aircraft, with one seaplane carrier and a destroyer damaged. Shortly after the battle the

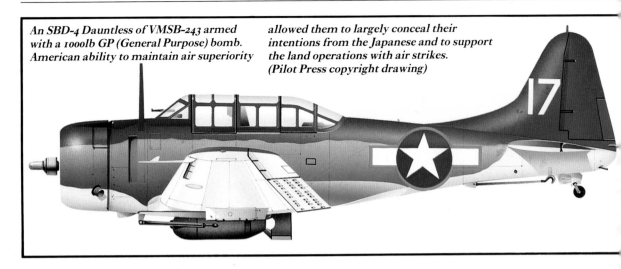

An SBD-4 Dauntless of VMSB-243 armed with a 1000lb GP (General Purpose) bomb. American ability to maintain air superiority allowed them to largely conceal their intentions from the Japanese and to support the land operations with air strikes. (Pilot Press copyright drawing)

American naval force départed. The Americans had sustained damage to one aircraft carrier, *Enterprise*, and had lost twenty planes. Far more serious losses followed. On 31 August, the aircraft carrier *Saratoga*, patrolling west of the Santa Cruz Islands, was torpedoed. The aircraft carrier *Wasp*, on patrol south-east of the Solomons, was torpedoed and sunk on 15 September. The battleship *North Carolina* was also torpedoed at the same time by a torpedo launched from the same spread that hit *Wasp*. The waters in this region were known, thereafter, as 'Torpedo Junction'. With one carrier sunk and two damaged, *Hornet* was the only American aircraft carrier in the South Pacific.

The Second Battle of the Matanikau

The last action during the month of August was a land battle. A second action was planned by the 5th Marines and was designed to place the 1st Battalion, 5th Marines, ashore west of Point Cruz. The mission of this battalion remains unclear: the battalion commander was given verbal orders and did not disclose them in their entirety to his staff.

The battalion landed unopposed at 0730 on 27 August. Because of the narrowness of the coast in that region and thick jungle terrain, the movement of the battalion was slowed and channelized. Steep ridges overlooked the battalion's route of march, and covering troops had to be placed on them to secure the flanks. But within a short time it became apparent that the security force could not keep pace with the main body. All contact between the two groups was physical, owing to an absence of squad-type radios. The terrain eventually wore down the covering force, necessitating relief. Once this was accomplished, the battalion continued to a point along the coast where the coral ridge narrowed the coastal plain down to 200 yards wide. Here the Japanese opened fire from concealed dug-in positions.

The leading company began to take casualties as it attempted to deploy. A second company was ordered to make a flanking movement towards the north-east as the endangered company made an assault from the west. This attack was supported by weapons from a third company. But the terrain and climate proved too much for such a manoeuvre, and the attack bogged down. Realizing that he could not dislodge the Japanese defenders from their strongpoint, and that further unsupported attacks would cause unnecessary deaths, the battalion commander requested permission to withdraw. The regimental commander, Colonel Hunt, relieved the battalion commander, placing the executive officer in charge.

Colonel Hunt then went down to the battle area and began to supervise the operation directly. He dictated that the battalion would remain in the field, and that the Japanese would continue to be attacked until defeated. The attack was launched the next morning – and met no opposition. The Japanese had withdrawn during the night. The battalion moved by coastal road to Matanikau village, where it was picked up by boat and taken back to the Lunga Perimeter.

SEPTEMBER

While the ground fighting was going on, important strategic developments were taking place. A Marine air wing was beginning to establish itself at Henderson Field. On 3 September 1942, the 1st Marine Aircraft Wing, under Brigadier General Roy S. Geiger, arrived. Geiger and his staff immediately reported to General Vandegrift and established a cooperative rapport that was to remain continuous throughout the campaign.

The conditions for air operations out of Henderson Field were as primitive as they could possibly be. However, like their fellow Marines in the Division, the Wing was soon to adapt to the conditions on the ground and to take control of the air war. In fact, with the arrival of the Wing, the tide in the air would eventually be turned against the Japanese pilots.

The Tasimboko Raid

After the Tenaru battle there were no major engagements until mid-September. However, there were reports from natives at the end of August that two to three hundred Japanese were fortifying the village of Tasimboko, about eight miles east of Lunga Point. In early September, the natives reported there were now several thousand

The pagoda-like structure set on a small hill overlooking Henderson Field became the operations centre for the airfield. It was equipped with a ground-to-air radio system that allowed the pagoda to contact planes on station and vector them towards incoming Japanese aircraft. (USMC 50032)

As the Marines began to improve their existing environment, the Pagoda was also improved and made into a usable shelter. A radio tunnel network was dug into the hill under the Pagoda so that operations could be shifted there in case of air raid or bombardment. Eventually the structure was torn down when General Vandegrift concluded that the Japanese were using it

as an aiming point to shell and bomb the airfield. (USMC 51812).

Japanese occupying that area. These reports were dismissed by Marine intelligence, but as a precautionary measure it was decided that an amphibious raid should be made against what was believed to be a small Japanese garrison force.

The Marines selected for the raid were from the 1st Raider Battalion and the 1st Parachute Battalion, who had recently been brought over from Tulagi. These two units had been formed into a composite battalion as a result of combat losses and were placed under the command of Lieutenant Colonel Merrit A. Edson. To conduct the raid they would sail on destroyer transports from the Lunga area to a point east of Tasimboko. Due to a shipping shortage, the Raiders would be landed first and the ships would return for the Parachutists.

The Raiders landed at dawn 8 September, followed shortly afterwards by the Parachutists. As they moved west they met minimal resistance until

▲ Major General Kawaguchi (seated, centre) with his staff officers. The picture was probably taken in the Philippines. Kawaguchi landed near Tasimbogo from destroyers on 6 September. Two days later he was attacked by Raiders and Parachutists as he made his way into the jungle. He was to meet the Marines again on 'Bloody Ridge'. Kawaguchi was defeated and his brigade destroyed. (National Archives)

they approached Tasimboko, when resistance sharply increased. The Japanese troops, estimated at 1,000, were well armed and equipped. They were also supported by field artillery firing at point-blank range. In order to continue the attack Edson set in motion an enveloping movement from the south. Using the Parachutists as rear and flank security, the Raiders initiated the attack and eventually, with air support from Henderson Field, the Japanese were forced from the village.

After occupying the village the attacking Marines discovered thousands of life jackets and enough supplies to feed as many troops as there were life jackets. What they did not know was that the Japanese they had just fought were the rear party of the 35th Infantry Regiment (or Kawaguchi Brigade, as it was referred to). Totalling more than 3,000 Japanese commanded by Major General Kiyotaki Kawaguchi, it had arrived between 29 August and 1 September.

Two events saved the smaller Marine force from being destroyed by the larger Japanese force. First was the fact that Kawaguchi had already formed his command to move south-west through the jungle. His intention was to move undetected to the south of Henderson Field and then launch an attack north from the jungle. Second, an American resupply convoy en route to Lunga Point was passing by the area. The Japanese incorrectly concluded that the convoy was reinforcing the Marine attacking force and a full-scale landing was being made. Kawaguchi and Edson would meet again, less than a week later, on a grassy ridge overlooking Henderson Field.

The Battle of 'Bloody Ridge'

After Tasimboko it was decided to put the Raiders and Parachutists in a reserve position. They were to occupy a defensive position on a series of grassy ridges south of Henderson Field, near the Division command post.

Patrols and native scouts that frequented the area south of Henderson Field began to encounter increasing Japanese opposition. Small artillery pieces were often located at various sites within range of the Marine perimeter, and on 10 September native scouts reported that the Japanese were cutting a trail from the east and were about five miles from the Perimeter. All these indicators pointed to the fact that a major Japanese offensive was in the making.

On 12 September, the Raiders attempted to patrol south of their position and encountered unexpected Japanese resistance. To add emphasis to the Japanese presence in the area, the ridge positions were bombed in a daily air raid. Unable to advance, they consolidated their positions on the southernmost knoll of the ridge complex. This would be the start of a crucial battle that would be called the Battle of 'Bloody Ridge' – a decided turning point in the campaign.

To defend the area, Edson positioned his composite battalion of Raiders and Parachutists in a linear defence along the southernmost ridge and in the surrounding jungle. The western flank was

General Vandegrift's tent near 'Bloody Ridge'. Because of the frequent shelling of Henderson Field, General Vandegrift moved his command post out to a quieter area in early September. He then had the Raiders moved on to the ridge near his position to cover the southern end of the perimeter. It was thought that this area was a quiet sector and would not see much action. Immediately after the battle, Vandegrift relocated his command post back to the Henderson Field area. (USMC 50489)

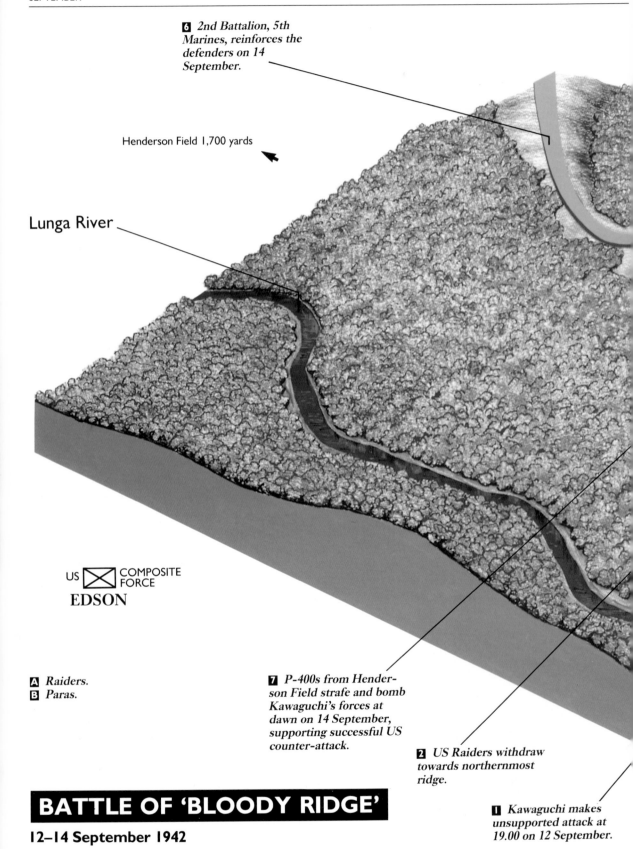

6 *2nd Battalion, 5th Marines, reinforces the defenders on 14 September.*

Henderson Field 1,700 yards

Lunga River

US ⊠ COMPOSITE FORCE

EDSON

A Raiders.
B Paras.

7 *P-400s from Henderson Field strafe and bomb Kawaguchi's forces at dawn on 14 September, supporting successful US counter-attack.*

2 *US Raiders withdraw towards northernmost ridge.*

BATTLE OF 'BLOODY RIDGE'

12–14 September 1942

1 *Kawaguchi makes unsupported attack at 19.00 on 12 September.*

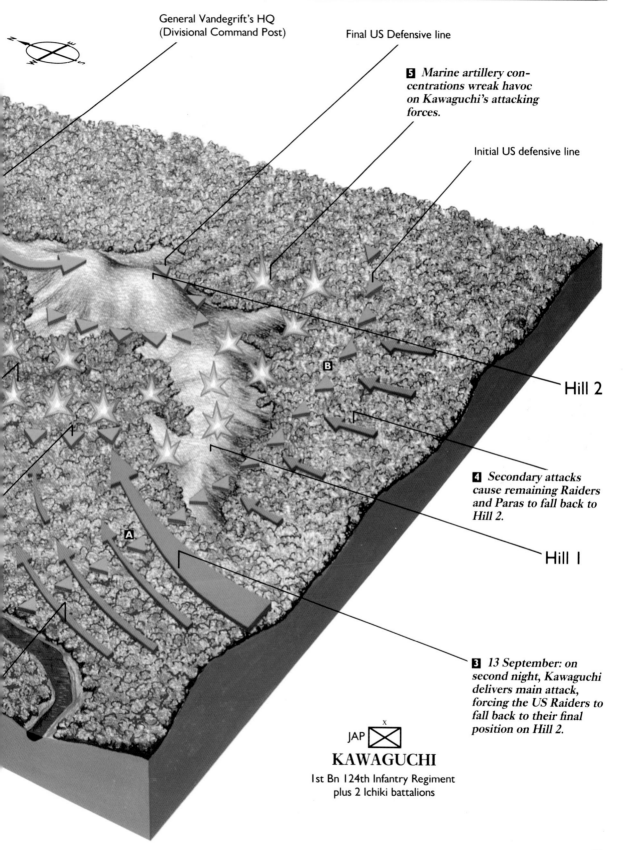

General Vandegrift's HQ
(Divisional Command Post)

Final US Defensive line

5 *Marine artillery concentrations wreak havoc
on Kawaguchi's attacking
forces.*

Initial US defensive line

Hill 2

4 *Secondary attacks
cause remaining Raiders
and Paras to fall back to
Hill 2.*

Hill 1

3 *13 September: on
second night, Kawaguchi
delivers main attack,
forcing the US Raiders to
fall back to their final
position on Hill 2.*

JAP

KAWAGUCHI

1st Bn 124th Infantry Regiment
plus 2 Ichiki battalions

B

A

▲ This is a view of the southernmost portion of 'Bloody Ridge'. It was here that Kawaguchi struck the Marines repeatedly from the thick jungle seen to the south. The Marines held a linear defensive position that stretched off to the left of this photograph. In the determined attacks, the Marines were pushed back north towards the airfield. (USMC 54970)

▼The thick jungle is clearly evident in this picture. Here we see a Marine scanning it for signs of Japanese movement. Should any activity be detected, it can be forwarded on the field telephone seen immediately behind the Marine. This photograph was taken on top of 'Bloody Ridge', and Mount Austen can be seen in the right background. (USMC 61547)

▲The southern ridge line. This picture shows a connecting trench to a covered machine-gun position located on the military crest of the forward slope. The thick jungle is present in the foreground. It was from the jungle that the Japanese attack came. Mount Austen looms on the horizon. (USMC 53094)

▼Edson's final position was the northernmost ridge seen in the background. Had it fallen on the night of 13/14 September there would have been nothing to stop the Japanese from advancing to Henderson Field. This picture was taken from the southern ridge looking north. (USMC 5000)

Conditions on Guadalcanal were equally appalling for Japanese and Americans alike. The Japanese lost around 9000 men from disease and starvation during the campaign. (Shirley Mallinson)

anchored on the Lunga River. The attack began that evening with shelling from Japanese warships, followed by repeated probings of the Marine lines from the jungle to the south. Later that night the numerically superior Kawaguchi Brigade repeatedly struck the Marines. The attack was preceded by a 20-minute naval bombardment, followed by a flare fired just forward of the Marine lines. As the flare faded away, Kawaguchi ordered his troops to initiate their attack. Powerful thrusts were directed from the west primarily against the companies that occupied the jungle terrain flanking the ridge. The Raiders were pushed back, and at times there was danger of some of the flanking companies being cut off.

The next day, 13 September, Edson attempted to use his reserve companies to dislodge the Japanese who had established a western salient into his position. This daylight attack did not meet with success, so Edson ordered his Marines to prepare and improve existing positions while waiting for the inevitable night attack. Throughout the day Japanese planes attacked the Lunga Perimeter, sometimes bombing the ridge.

The second night, Kawaguchi struck with two infantry battalions. He succeeded in driving the Marines back to the northernmost knoll of the ridge. From this final position the Marines held back the Japanese onslaught. Kawaguchi struck twelve times, each attack being preceded by rocket flares. The fighting was fierce, each side sensing the importance of the terrain feature they were holding or fighting for. Kawaguchi knew that he would have to overwhelm the Raiders and Parachutists if his attack on Henderson field were to succeed; Edson knew that at this stage of the battle his troops were no longer just fighting to save Henderson Field – they were fighting to save their very lives.

The flares fired by Kawaguchi's troops served as a signal for his troops to attack and also indicated the direction of attack, which made an excellent reference point for Marine artillery fire. With their guns firing direct support at close range, the defending Marines were able to hold.

At dawn on 14 September, planes from Henderson Field and the 2nd Battalion, 5th Marines supported the Raiders and Parachutists in driving

▲ *This picture was taken near the aid station on 'Bloody Ridge'. Had this last northern ridge fallen, the Japanese would have been able to advance down the dirt road in the rear of the picture to Henderson Field. The closeness of the jungle to this ridge and its seemingly impenetrable nature caused the Marines to think the Japanese would not attack the perimeter from this southerly direction. (USMC 50003)*

▼ *This is the road that leads from 'Bloody Ridge' to the airport. In this picture it is very easy to see why the defence of 'Bloody Ridge' was so critical. Once the Japanese advanced to the open plain in the foreground, they would have seized the airfield and driven a deadly wedge between the Marine forces. Had the Japanese succeeded, there is some doubt whether they could have been ejected. (USMC 52059)*

the remainder of Kawaguchi's forces back into the jungle. Kawaguchi had been defeated; the majority of his troops were either dead or dying in the jungle or on the slopes of the ridge that overlooked Henderson Field.

In the Battle of 'Bloody Ridge', the Marines had achieved a significant victory over a superior Japanese force and undoubtedly saved Henderson Field from capture. The Marines lost 31 killed, 103 wounded and nine missing; the Japanese lost more than 600 killed. For his heroic defence on 'Bloody Ridge', Edson, along with one of his company commanders, Major Kenneth D. Bailey, would receive the Congressional Medal of Honor.

While Kawaguchi was attacking at 'Bloody Ridge', a second unit of his force, about two companies, attacked The 3rd Battalion 1st Marines at 'Alligator Creek'. A fight developed that lasted through the night but the Marines repulsed it decisively. A third attack, probably led by Colonel Oka's command, struck the 3rd Battalion, 5th Marines from the west. This attack was also repulsed.

September Matanikau Action

With all the Japanese attacks repulsed, General Vandegrift decided to expand the Marine perimeter. Bolstered by the addition of the 7th Marines, recently transported from Samoa, Vandegrift tasked them with clearing the Japanese from the Matanikau area. The action was planned initially to be accomplished in two separate phases. A reconnaissance in force this time by the 1st Battalion, 7th Marines, was to be conducted from 23-26 September in the area between Mount Austen and Kokumbona. On 27 September, the 1st Raiders Battalion was to conduct an attack at the mouth of the Matanikau River with the objective of pushing through to Kokumbona and establishing a patrol base there.

The 1st Battalion, Seventh Marines, under the command of Lieutenant Colonel Lewis B. 'Chesty' Puller, set out for the Mount Austen area on 23 September. During that day, no contact with the Japanese was made. Late in the evening of the following day, however, the battalion made contact with a strong Japanese force near Mount Austen. In the ensuing action, which was broken off at nightfall, the battalion sustained seven killed and 25 wounded. Puller's Marines planned to continue the attack the next day, but requested to evacuate all their wounded before attacking again. General Vandegrift, fearing that Puller had made contact with a strong Japanese force, sent the 2nd Battalion, 5th Marines, to reinforce him. With the increase in forces, Puller was able to detach two of his companies to escort the wounded back to the Marine lines.

The combined force then continued its advance to clear the east bank of the Mantanikau. As it approached the river mouth on 26 September, the combined force was taken under fire by the Japanese from the west bank and the controlling western ridges. The 2nd Battalion, 5th Marines succeeded in making its way to the mouth of the river, but could not force a crossing. It was decided to have Puller's Marines and the 2nd Battalion, 5th Marines hold and engage the Japanese at the mouth of the river.

The 1st Raider Battalion, meanwhile, had set out from the Perimeter to accomplish its portion of the overall mission. However, developments at the Matanikau River caused their plan of operation to be altered. The Raiders would move up the east bank of the river, cross at a spot where that river forked about 2,000 yards upstream, and strike the Japanese from the right rear. The action began early on 27 September 1942 with the Raiders, now under Lieutenant Colonel Sam Griffith (Edson having been promoted and given command of the 5th Marines), moving up to their intended crossing point. As it moved into position, the unit discovered that a sizable enemy force had crossed the river and had taken up strong positions on the east bank.

Fighting soon erupted and Griffith was wounded. His new executive officer, Major Bailey (who had won the Medal of Honor on 'Bloody Ridge') was killed. The concentrated fire of the Japanese from the front flanks succeeded not only in stopping the assault but in preventing the Raiders deploying. From this point on, the American operation degenerated. A message from the Raiders was interpreted incorrectly at Division headquarters, and it was erroneously inferred that the Raiders had successfully crossed the river.

In order to assist them, it was decided to send out the two companies from Puller's battalion in a shore-to-shore landing. Their mission was to cut off any retreating Japanese and assist the units fighting at the Matanikau. Naval gunfire support would be provided on this portion of the operation by the destroyer *Ballard*. The landing was to be made in two waves west of Point Cruz but did not receive the requested fire support from the destroyer, the result of an earlier air raid that disrupted fire support communications. Fortunately the landing was unopposed.

The first opposition came in the form of mortar bombs, which fell on the Marines just as they reached the ridges 500 yards south of the landing beach. One of the first bombs to fall killed Major Otho L. Rogers, the battalion executive officer, who was commanding this phase of the operation. To make matters worse, a strong enemy column was observed coming from the Matanikau River, and this began to engage the Marines. Now all three Marine forces were in combat with the Japanese but unable to support each other.

The most serious threat was directed at the force that had landed west of Point Cruz. It was in danger of being surrounded. Unfortunately, radio equipment had not been brought ashore, and the Division command post was not aware of what was happening. This situation was quickly rectified when the Marines spelled out the word 'HELP' with their T-shirts. The message was spotted by a dive-bomber pilot, Lieutenant Dale M. Leslie, who radioed a message to the 5th Marines.

Puller, who had been with the Matanikau force, now realized how serious the situation was and left the Matanikau area to rescue his isolated companies. Securing permission to take a small flotilla of landing craft up the coast, Puller set out on the rescue mission. En route, he came across the destroyer, *Ballard*, which he hailed down and boarded. This small task force then continued towards the beleaguered Marines.

When *Ballard* showed up on station, its fire direction centre could not communicate with the Marines on shore, so fire support was not immediately available. In order to signal to the ship, Sergeant Robert D. Raysbrook, exposed himself to Japanese fire. Standing up on the ridge, Raysbrook

▶ *This is the terrain on the east bank of the Matanikau that Lieutenant Colonel Puller's Marines operated in as they swept north to clear the east bank in late September 1942. The Matanikau River can be seen through the trees slightly left of centre. (USMC 116749)*

Guadalcanal represented the first use in a combat zone of the LVT-1 (Landing Vehicle Tracked), popularly known as the 'Alligator'.

The amtracs of the 1st and 2nd Amphibian Tractor Battalions provided logistical support for the landings. (Terry Hadler)

began semaphoring fire directions to *Ballard*. (For his heroism, he was to be awarded the Navy Cross, as well as a comparable award by Great Britain.) As the Marines withdrew from the ridge, under the cover of naval gunfire, Platoon Sergeant Anthony P. Malinowski, Jr., single-handedly covered their withdrawal with a Browning Automatic Rifle until he was killed, an action that earned him a Navy Cross.

Once the Marines reached the beach, they set up a hasty defence and waited for the approaching landing craft. Japanese fire from Point Cruz to the east and Kokumbona to the west then began to hit the approaching landing craft, causing casualties.

Lieutenant Leslie, who had remained in the air over the area in his dive-bomber, flew low over the landing craft and strafed Japanese positions on the beach. Also in this action, a Coast Guard Signalman 1st Class, Douglas Munro, manning a machine-gun on one of the landing craft, began to engage the Japanese. For his heroic lifesaving actions under fire, he became the only Coast Guardsman to win the Medal of Honor.

The companies were finally evacuated at a cost of 24 killed and 23 wounded. The Japanese force the Marines came into contact with was estimated to be 1,800 strong and had lost 60 killed and 100 wounded. Once the withdrawal was accomplished, the Marines along the Matanikau also pulled back to the Perimeter, leaving the Japanese still in control of the region and ending the ground fighting for the month of September.

The naval actions during the month were limited to the nightly attempts to interdict the 'Tokyo Express'.

▶ *In early October the Japanese, using long range artillery, began to bombard Henderson Field. Weapons such as this 105mm artillery piece, with its battery headquarters located near White River west of Point Cruz, disrupted airfield operation. The Marine attack in the Matanika area in early October struck the Japanese just as they were preparing to launch an attack. The purpose for the Japanese attack was to secure the east bank of the Matanikau for firing positions for these types of artillery pieces. The Marines referred to the Japanese artillery as 'Pistol Pete'. (USMC)*

OCTOBER

Early in October a Marine Raider patrol reported a Japanese build up in the east, near Gurabusu and Koilotumaria, two native villages lying between Lunga and Aola. The Americans concluded that the Japanese in the area were possibly planning another attack from the east. To counter this suspected attack it was decided to bring the 1st Battalion, 2nd Marines, over from Tulagi and to make a shore to shore landing. The target date for the landing was 9 October. The crossing was made in Higgins boats towed by larger landing craft. The operation was marred when one of the Higgins boats' bow assembly pulled loose during tow. The boat sank immediately, drowning 18 Marines and sailors. Subsequent rescue operations delayed the landing and caused operational plans to be changed.

Koilotumaria was attacked first on 10 October and no opposition was met. However, the Marines did discover positions for more than 200 Japanese in the area. At Gurabusu, which was attacked two hours later, some opposition was met and over-come. The Japanese lost 30 killed and the Marines lost one killed and one wounded. A large amount of supplies were captured and destroyed, but the main Japanese force was not located. All indications pointed to the fact that the Japanese forces in the area had moved south into the jungle and would possibly link up with existing Japanese forces on Guadalcanal.

October Matanikau Battle

October was a busy month for both sides. The Americans wanted to drive the Japanese from their Matanikau stronghold, and intelligence reports indicated that the Japanese were massing in the region for another all-out attack. To add credence to these reports, recently landed Japanese artillery, nicknamed 'Pistol Pete', was beginning to range in on Henderson Field, interrupting airfield operations.

General Vandegrift initiated a plan of attack that called for the 5th Marines (minus one

battalion) to conduct a spoiling attack at the mouth of the Matanikau River, which would focus Japanese attention on that area; meanwhile the 7th Marines, (minus one battalion), reinforced by the 3rd Battalion, 2nd Marines, would cross the river upstream, then turn north to clear the area on the west bank. The operation would be supported by artillery and from the air. The objective of the attack was to establish a line far enough to the west to prohibit Japanese artillery from firing at Henderson Field.

The Japanese had prepared a similar plan. The 4th Infantry Regiment, under Colonel Tadamasu Nakaguma, was to seize positions east of the Matanikau River. By doing this the Japanese would be able to establish better positions for their artillery while denying the Marines their Matanikau line.

Fortunately for the Marines, they put their plan into action first. The battle lasted from 7 to 9 October; the plan of attack roughly followed the previous month's aborted attack in the Matanikau region. The plan called for the 5th Marines to set up positions on the east bank of the Matanikau running south from the mouth by 1,800 yards. The main force, composed of the 3rd Battalion, 2nd

◀ The terrain the Marines moved through in the Matanikau region was hardly passable. Often the point elements had to blaze a trail through tangled terrain, and progress was extremely limited. In this picture, a machine-gun crew struggles to get its ammunition cart up a slight slope. Working like this in the heat and humidity sapped the endurance of the Marines. (USMC A 702876)

Marines, plus a scout-sniper group commanded by Colonel William J. Whaling, and the 7th Marines would cross the Matanikau at its upstream fork and move northwards. It would then cross the high ground south of Matanikau village and assault the village. The attack formation would have Whaling's group secure the high ground overlooking the west bank. The 7th Marines would operate on the high ground just to the west of Whaling and seize the high ground south-west of Point Cruz, cutting off any retreating Japanese. 8 October was the date set for the operation.

On 7 October the advance began. By noon, the 3rd Battalion, 5th Marines, had made contact with a company sized Japanese unit east of the river and a short distance inland from the river's mouth. The Marines began to drive the Japanese back and contained a large number of them on the east bank. The Japanese then launched several strong counterattacks, all of which were beaten back.

Next day the Raiders were fed into the lines to reinforce the 3rd Battalion, 5th Marines. That night, the Japanese attacked again: at 1830 there was one final attack the brunt of which was taken by the Raiders. Heavy hand-to-hand fighting took place, but in the end the Raiders won. They lost 12 killed and 22 wounded; the Japanese lost 60 killed.

The main attack, which was held back until 9 October because of torrential rain, was now launched. The Whaling group crossed the river quickly, occupied the high ground west of the river and pushed north along the west bank. The 7th Marines followed and were equally successful.

The 1st Battalion, 7th Marines, led by Lieutenant Colonel Puller was operating at the most westerly point of the operation when it came across a large concentration of Japanese from the 4th Infantry Regiment camped in a deep ravine. Calling for artillery support and using all available mortars and weapons, Puller's battalion poured a deadly fire upon the Japanese trapped in the ravine, a process of elimination that continued until ammunition was exhausted. In the fighting the Marines killed more than 700 Japanese with a cost to themselves of 65 killed and 125 wounded. They withdraw from the area when word of an impending counter-offensive was received.

The Japanese Counter-Offensive

The Japanese, who had been planning a full scale counter-offensive since August, had completed new preparations by October. Their first attempts by the Ichiki and Kawaguchi Brigades had met with failure, essentially because they had underestimated the troop strength of the Americans and had sent forces that were numerically insufficient. The October counter-offensive directed by General Hyakutake, who commanded the 17th Army, called for elaborate plans to recapture Guadalcanal. In a joint Army-Navy operation, two army divisions, the 2nd (Sendai) and the 38th, were used to augment 17th Army units. All existing Japanese units on Guadalcanal would also be used in this all-out effort.

The Battle of Cape Esperance

This major counter-offensive was to be launched on three fronts. The first phase began at sea, with the Battle of Cape Esperance. In this battle the opposing naval forces made contact near Savo Island. The Americans under Rear Admiral Norman Scott took up a north–south position against the Japanese force that was moving at a right-angle towards it. Admiral Scott then executed a classic crossing the 'T' manoeuvre, the main batteries of the American ships being brought to bear on the Japanese ships, which were travelling in a line-ahead formation that restricted their return fire. As a result of this engagement the Japanese were forced to retire. On each side a destroyer was lost and a cruiser damaged. It was not a major victory, but the naval balance of power was starting to shift towards the Americans.

The Battle For Henderson Field

The victory at Cape Esperance was short lived. On 13 October 1942, the Japanese struck Henderson Field with an intense aerial bombardment, causing damage so severe that the airfield could be used only for emergency landings. No sooner had the last Japanese aircraft departed than Japanese 150mm howitzers located near Kokumbona opened fire. The Marines did not have an effective

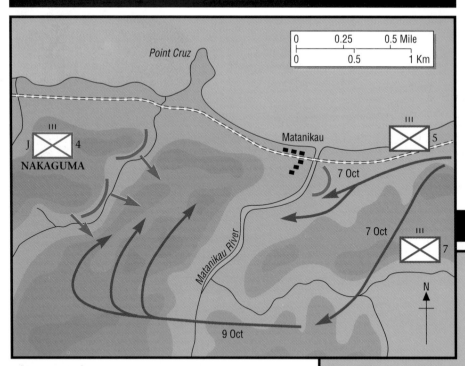

The Matanikau Offensive of 7-9 October 1942

▶ *Damage wreaked on Henderson Field by battleships in mid-October. The constant bombardment by the Japanese, coupled with aerial bombing, virtually closed down the field to all but emergency operations. With the field virtually knocked out, the Japanese believed they could take Guadalcanal with ease. (USMC 61548)*

The Battle f

counter-battery weapon with which to engage the Japanese. The attack continued throughout the day. Shortly before midnight – in a night that would be remembered as the 'Night of the Battleships' – two Japanese battleships, *Haruna* and *Kongo*, began a systematic bombardment of Henderson Field. When they retired, bombers hit the airfield again. By the afternoon of 14 October, Henderson Field was completely out of action. Air operations were shifted over to a rough grassy runway to the south-east; but on this strip, Fighter Strip No 1, only minimal operations could be carried out.

On 15 October, five Japanese transports covered by their screening warships began to unload troops and supplies at Tassafaronga Point, ten miles to the west. The Americans managed to put up a few planes and, coupled with American Army bombers from Espirito Santo in the New Hebrides, managed to sink one transport and set two on fire. The Japanese were forced to retire, but not before they had landed between 3,000 and 4,000 troops and 80 per cent of their cargo.

With the arrival of the last of his troops, General Hyakutake was confident of success.

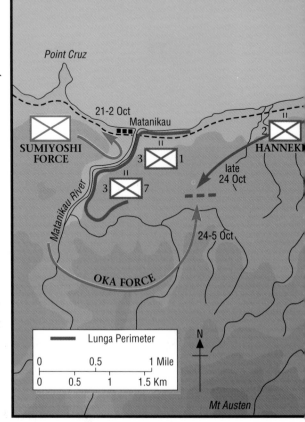

nderson Field, 23-5 October 1942

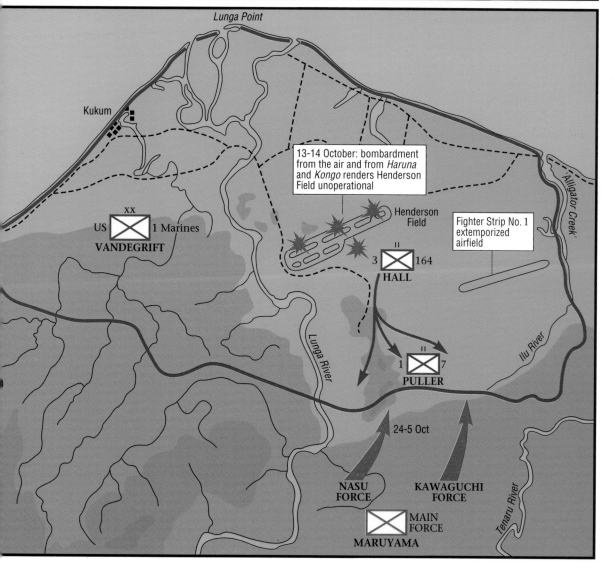

Lunga Point

Kukum

13-14 October: bombardment from the air and from *Haruna* and *Kongo* renders Henderson Field unoperational

Henderson Field

Fighter Strip No. 1 extemporized airfield

US ⊠ 1 Marines
VANDEGRIFT

3 ⊠ 164
HALL

1 ⊠ 7
PULLER

Lunga River

'Alligator Creek'

Ilu River

24-5 Oct

NASU FORCE

KAWAGUCHI FORCE

⊠ MAIN FORCE
MARUYAMA

Tenaru River

▲ With Henderson Field virtually out of commission, operations were shifted to a muddy fighter strip located north-east of Henderson. Here, planes could take off and land, making a few sorties a day until Henderson was operational. In this photograph a group of F4F-4s are readied for take off from Fighter Strip No 1. (USMC 52801)

Indeed, so confident were the Japanese that they had drawn up a surrender plan, which entailed General Vandegrift, along with his staff officers and interpreters, advancing along the north coast road. They would carry one American flag and a white surrender flag. The surrender would take place at the mouth of the Matanikau River. Once the surrender was accomplished, the code name, 'Banzai', would be signalled to herald the success.

The plan of attack was to be four-pronged. Lieutenant General Maruyama was to lead the main force and attack from the south, near 'Bloody Ridge'; Major General Kawaguchi's force would attack from the south-east between, 'Alligator Creek' and 'Bloody Ridge'; Major General Nasu would attack from the south-west, between the Lunga River and 'Bloody Ridge'. The second prong, under Major General Sumiyoshi, was to attack from the west with tank support and cross the Matanikau River. The third prong, under Colonel Oka, was to cross the Matanikau River a mile upstream and move north against the Marines occupying a series of ridges east of the river. The fourth prong called for an amphibious assault at Koli Point; in the event this was cancelled when the Japanese believed American resistance was about to collapse.

The attack was to commence on 22 October; however, movement through the jungle caused unexpected delays – delays that upset a very elaborately coordinated attack schedule. The route of march selected by General Maruyama, called the 'Maruyama Trail', led through some of the thickest jungle on Guadalcanal. Having no engineering equipment, the Japanese were forced to hack through the jungle with hand tools. All supplies had to be manpacked, and the artillery pieces were the first to be left along the tortuous trail that made its way up and down the steep slopes south of Mount Austen. In a single file column that inched along, Maruyama was unable to maintain his schedule: by 22 October he had to postpone his attack to the 23rd; on the 23rd, he postponed it to the 24th.

Meanwhile General Sumiyoshi, who was out of communication with Maruyama, began his attack on the afternoon of 21 October. The attack started with increased artillery fire directed against the 3rd Battalion, 1st Marines, holding the east bank of the Matanikau River. Immediately after the artillery fired, a strong patrol accompanied by nine tanks attempted to cross the sand bar. They were driven back with the loss of one tank.

The following day was quiet until 1800. Then the Japanese attacked again. Once again artillery bombarded the Marines, and tanks, followed by a massive troop attack, struck the Marine lines. The Marines were ready. Artillery from ten batteries of the 11th Marines and a concentration of anti-tank weaponry waited for the Japanese. The concentrated fire of the supporting arms wreaked havoc with the Japanese attack. The massed Marine artillery fire virtually annihilated Sumiyoshi's troops and destroyed three of his tanks in an assembly area; nine others were destroyed by anti-tank weapons and were left burning on the sand bar. Sumiyoshi had been defeated; the Marines had held the western sector.

The following night, 24 October, in the middle of a blinding rain storm, Maruyama's forces launched their attack against the 1st Battalion, 7th Marines, commanded by Lieutenant Colonel Puller. The attack began about 2130 in the evening when a Marine listening post opened fire on the advance elements of the Japanese 29th Infantry Regiment and retreated. Their movement was shielded by a blinding rain storm. The Japanese, under Maruyama, had finally hacked their way through the jungle to the south of the Marines and were launching their attack. They had crossed the upper reaches of the Lunga River and were now just south of 'Bloody Ridge'. To support their attacks they had nothing more than machine-guns; all the artillery and mortars had been abandoned

Lieutenant General Masao Maruyama, Commanding General of the Second (Sendai) Division, attacked the Marine perimeter from the south in October. Maruyama's troops, using and tools, cut a trail through the torturous jungle but were not unable to maintain the planned attack timetable. The result was an uncoordinated attack that was defeated. (USMC)

A detailed view of one of General Sumiyoshi's light battle tanks as it sinks into the sand. The defeat of Sumiyoshi's forces in the west destroyed a third of the Japanese forces committed to the October offensive. (Signal Corps 63893)

along the 'Maryuama Trail'. Maruyama had hoped for bright moonlight to orientate his troops, but the clouds and rain made the night black. The clash with the outpost was unavoidable and tipped off the Americans. The front lines were quiet for about two hours until suddenly the 29th Infantry attacked Puller's battalion east of 'Bloody Ridge'.

Simultaneous with Maryuama's attack was Colonel Oka's attack on the south-western side of the Marine perimeter. Marine planners at Division headquarters correctly assessed that Maryuama's attack was the main effort and immediately ordered the 7th Marines reserve force (3rd Battalion, 164th Infantry) to reinforce Puller. The battalion, under Lieutenant Colonel Robert K. Hall, had only recently arrived on Guadalcanal, and were in bivouac south of Henderson Field, about a mile from Puller. With rain falling heavily, and with poor visibility, Hall's battalion marched out to link up with Puller. The Marines continued to hold, and Hall's battalion was guided into their position. The two battalions did not defend separate sectors but were intermingled along the front lines. The Japanese resolutely attacked during the night, but every charge was beaten back by the Marines and soldiers.

The following day, 25 October, became known as 'Dugout Sunday'. The Japanese continually shelled and bombed Henderson Field in one of the heaviest concentrations to date. The Marines reorganized their lines and waited for the night, which would bring on the inevitable Japanese attacks. Maruyama struck the Marines as he had the previous night. His 16th and 29th Infantry Regiments attacked savagely along the southern portion of 'Bloody Ridge'. Again the Marines and soldiers, supported by Marine 37mm anti-tank weapons firing canister rounds, repulsed the final assault.

One Marine who distinguished himself throughout this action was Platoon Sergeant 'Manila John' Basilone, who, operating in imminent danger and constantly exposing himself to hostile fire, kept the machine-guns in his section of the front lines operating under almost impossible conditions. For his constant feats of heroism in this action he was to be awarded the Congressional Medal of Honor.

At dawn Maruyama withdrew, leaving more than 1,500 of his troops dead in front of the Marine lines. Among the dead were General Nasu and Colonels Furumiya and Hiroyasu (commanding the 29th and 16th Regiments, respectively).

Also on 25 October, Colonel Oka's force attacked the 2nd Battalion, 7th Marines on the ridges east of the Matanikau River. In a fierce night battle, Oka's forces also met with defeat. The battle began shortly after the 2nd Battalion, 7th Marines, under Lieutenant Colonel Herman Hanneken, had been quickly moved into position on a ridge line near the Matanikau. They were positioned there to deny the Japanese an avenue of approach in case they should attempt to outflank the 3rd Battalion, 7th Marines, and 3rd Battalion 1st Marines, who were holding the Matanikau River line. Hanneken's battalion was in an exposed position: there was no continuous line, and the battalion did not tie in with the others. It occupied a position on a ridge formed by two hills whose long axis ran generally east–east, and was occupied by the Marines some time about 1830 on 24 October.

The battle began on the evening of 25 October 1942. During the night, numerous attempts at infiltration were made by Colonel Oka's troops who had been observed crossing Mount Austen's foothills the day before. Three separate attacks were made on the east flank at 2130, and at 2300 a battalion sized unit attacked. All these attacks were beaten back.

At 0300, under pressure of an overwhelming attack, the Marines on the eastern portion of the ridge, were pushed off, with the exception of one machine-gun team. Those on the western portion of the ridge fought back strongly, and before the Japanese could consolidate their hold a counterattack was launched, led by the battalion executive officer, Major Odell M. Conoley. Forming a composite group of Marines from the headquarters section, Conoley drove the Japanese back off the ridge.

Also during this action, a platoon sergeant by the name of Mitchell Paige won the Congressional Medal of Honor for holding the Japanese at bay as they overran the eastern portion of the ridge. By holding his position against seemingly insur-

General Sumiyoshi's attack across the Matinakau was supported by several Type 97 Chi-ha medium tanks of the 1st Independent Tank Company, which was formed from veteran crews of the 4th Company, 2nd Tank Regiment. (Steven J. Zaloga)

mountable odds. Paige was able to disrupt the Japanese and prevent them from outflanking the Marine positions. In a further heroic action, Paige led a group of Marines in an attack that broke the back of the final Japanese assault. In that attack, Paige cradled a .30 calibre water-cooled machine-gun in his arms as he ran forward firing it into the Japanese.

These unsuccessful Japanese attacks marked the end of their October counter-offensive. It would also be the high water mark for the Japanese in the campaign. Other battles, many just as fierce, were yet to be fought, but October would be the decisive month on land.

▶ *Conditions were so bad on Guadalcanal in October that General Vandegrift directed Lieutenant Colonel Twining, the Assistant Operations Officer, to prepare a secret withdrawal plan. The plan was set up to enable the Marines to withdraw from the Lunga area, fight a delaying action to the east and conduct guerrilla warfare from the hills to the south. Fortunately, the plan was never implemented. This picture shows Lieutenant Colonel Twining, in the foreground, at his desk in the operations section. (USMC 52548)*

The Battle of Santa Cruz

At sea, October ended with the Battle of the Santa Cruz Islands. In that battle, a strong Japanese force that had been manoeuvring in the area was attacked by a naval task force under Rear Admiral Thomas C. Kinkaid. The ensuing battle was a series of air-to-ship and air-to-air actions in which the Americans lost an aircraft carrier and a destroyer, while another aircraft carrier, a battleship, a cruiser and a destroyer were damaged. The Japanese lost no ships while sustaining damage to three aircraft carriers and two destroyers; but their forces departed the area.

▼*Henderson Field from the air. This picture taken in November shows the progress made on the airfield by the Americans. The main runway, which was improved by adding Martson steel matting and crushed coral, is evident. Also, taxi-ways to facilitate take-offs and landings have been added. In the middle background lie the foreboding grass covered slopes of Mount Austen, which was still in Japanese hands. (USMC 171864)*

▶*Admiral Halsey, who took over as commander of the South Pacific Area from Admiral Ghormley, is visited by Admiral Nimitz, Commander in Chief Pacific. (National Archives)*

NOVEMBER

November was a month of change in the campaign. The South Pacific Area received a new commander: Admiral Ghormley was relieved and Admiral William F. 'Bull' Halsey took command. Although Halsey officially assumed command on 20 October, he was not able to visit Guadalcanal until 8 November; but with Halsey came the much needed troops and supplies to maintain the American presence in the area.

The Naval Battle For Guadalcanal

The month was characterized by heavy naval actions. The Japanese organized four naval task forces for their November operations. Two bombardment forces were to shell Henderson Field; a third was to transport the 38th Division and its equipment to Guadalcanal; a fourth would be in general support.

The American naval forces under Halsey's command were organized into two task forces. One was led by Admiral Turner and the other by Admiral Kinkaid. These forces, although limited, had the task of reinforcing and resupplying Guadalcanal as well as stopping the Japanese from taking it over.

Admiral Kinkaid, who had the majority of warships, would cover Admiral Turner's amphibious force of warships and transports. Turner's force was subdivided into three groups: the first, led by Admiral Scott, would carry reinforcements to Guadalcanal; the second, led by Admiral Callaghan, would screen the third group. Admiral Turner would assume direct command of the third group, which was composed primarily of transports and carried critically needed supplies and reinforcements for Guadalcanal.

The groups arrived at the island and began resupply operations at 0530 on 12 November. At 1035 American aircraft reported a large Japanese naval force that included battleships sailing towards Guadalcanal. By late afternoon Turner had unloaded 90 per cent of his cargo and withdrew from the area, leaving Callaghan and Scott's forces to engage the Japanese.

The Japanese force, which had been spotted, consisted of the battleships *Hiei* and *Kirishima*, one light cruiser and fourteen destroyers. Their orders were to neutralize the airfields on Guadalcanal. Once the airfield had been put out of operation the Japanese could safely transport their troops to the island. The Japanese ships carried high-explosive shells for bombardment instead of armour piercing ammunition – which would later prove a blessing for the Americans once the two forces engaged. High-explosive shells reduced the effectiveness of the Japanese 14-inch guns, as the shells could not always penetrate the armour plate on the American cruisers.

In what would be called the First Battle for Guadalcanal, Admiral Callaghan led his outmatched cruiser force against the Japanese battleship force that was to bombard Henderson Field. The main action began at night near Savo Island. Callaghan's radar located the Japanese ships first. The vanguards of the opposing forces intermingled and the American column penetrated the Japanese formation; then a wild, confused mêlée began. The Japanese illuminated the American cruiser force and opened fire. The outnumbered Americans returned fire from all directions and the engagement degenerated into individual ship-to-ship actions. In the confusion both sides fired on their own ships. When the battle was over, Admirals Callaghan and Scott were dead, but the Japanese had been turned back. Not one Japanese shell had struck Guadalcanal. Of the thirteen American ships involved, twelve had been either sunk or damaged, while the Japanese had lost a battleship and two destroyers, with damage to four cruisers.

The November 1942 Battles on Guadalcanal

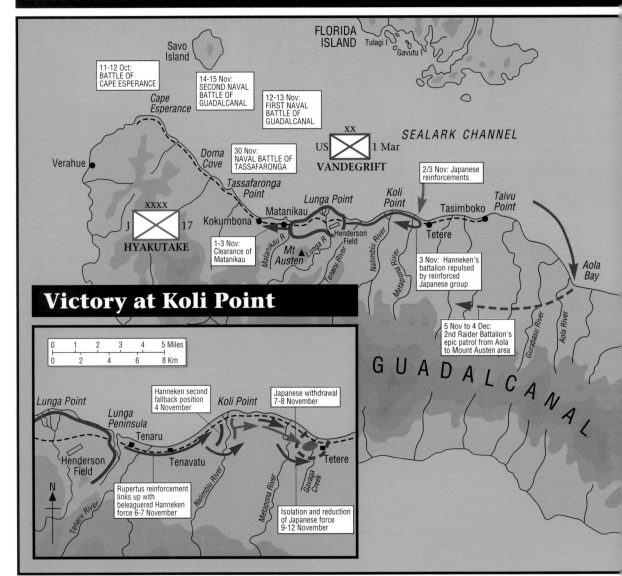

Victory at Koli Point

On 13 November, the Japanese attempted to reinforce Guadalcanal with a naval task force that included eleven transports. They were caught in the light the following day by both carrier and land based aircraft. Seven of the transports were sunk, and the four survivors continued toward Guadalcanal. Next day, they were discovered beached at Tassafaronga Point, there to be destroyed in short order by American aircraft, long range artillery and naval gunfire. Equally important as the destruction of the transports was the turning back of their screening force, which was to have bombarded Henderson Field.

November Matanikau Action

On land the situation was also improving. The 5th Marines spearheaded a western attack that cleared the Japanese out of the Matanikau area. Two other regiments, 2nd Marines less its 3rd Battalion but reinforced by the Army's 1st Battalion, 164th Infantry, continued the advance, stopping just short of Kokumbona.

This western plan of attack was essentially the same as all previous attacks in the Matanikau region. The 5th Marines supported by units of the

Lunga Perimeter
0   5   10 Miles
0   5   10   15 Km

N

▲*Prior to the 1 November attacks in the Matanikau region, Colonel Edson, now commanding the 5th Marine Regiment, speaks to his officers. Edson is seen here giving them a basic outline of upcoming events and future operations in the area. This setting is a captured Japanese building east of the Lunga River. (USMC)*

Division's Special Weapons Battalion, would attack west on a 1,500 yard frontage with two battalions abreast. The main attack was to be made along the high ground south of the coast. The 2nd Marines, who had recently arrived from Tulagi and were considered fresh, would follow up by advancing along the coastal plan. In order to protect the southern or inland flank, the 3rd Battalion, 7th Marines, would operate in force in that area. As a prelude to the attack, the 1st Engineer Battalion succeeded in erecting three makeshift bridges across the river.

The attack, which was preceded by an intense artillery and naval bombardment and supported by air strikes, began on schedule at 0700 on 1 November. The leading elements of the 5th Marines crossed the bridges and fanned out, moving into the hills overlooking the coast. There was no concentrated resistance in the area, and the advance continued into the early afternoon, with the 2nd Battalion, 5th Marines, advancing along the high ground to the west. As they pushed forward they met no determined resistance, but they soon lost contact with the 1st Battalion, 5th Marines, who were advancing west along the coast to the north.

As the 1st Battalion, 5th Marines, were making their advance they began to run into very stiff resistance from Japanese troops dug into a steep ravine located to the south. During the remainder of the day, the Americans maintained position facing the Japanese and were reinforced by the 3rd Battalion, 5th Marines.

Next day, 2 November, the two battalions began flanking movements that eventually boxed in the Japanese. Late in the afternoon, in a separate action, two companies from the 3rd Battalion, 5th Marines, ran into heavy opposition from a strong Japanese force concentrated between the coastal road and the beach. One of the companies, Company I, led by Captain Erskine Wells, launched the only documented bayonet charge of the campaign and routed the enemy.

In order to destroy the Japanese in the ravine, Marine half-tracks mounting 75mm guns were called up, but the terrain in the ravine was too rough for them to be deployed. The final phase of the attack was initiated at 0800 on the 3rd: the 2nd Battalion, 5th Marines, continued to attack the

◀Marines from the 5th Marines move up toward the Matanikau for the 1 November push. This attack would establish a Marine presence once and for all on the west bank of the Matanikau. The attack would take the Marines as far as the White River, which was to the west of Point Cruz. (USMC 51335)

◀This bridge was one of three constructed by the 1st Engineer Battalion to support the 1 November Marine attack. The bridges were constructed on the night of 31 October. Made out of fuel drum floats and other bridging materials, they were assembled and positioned quickly. The Marines crossing the bridge are part of the reserve force from the 2nd Battalion, 2nd Marine Regiment. (USMC 51337)

Japanese in the ravine until they were destroyed, the 1st Battalion, 164th Infantry, then assisting the Marines in mopping up bypassed pockets of resistance. The Japanese lost 239 killed during this action.

Action At Koli Point

On the opposite side of the Perimeter, the 7th Marines and the remainder of the 164th Infantry made an eastern push that drove the Japanese from the Koli Point area. This action was undertaken by the 2nd Battalion, 7th Marines, led by Lieutenant Colonel Herman H. Hanneken. The battalion was trucked east from the Tenaru River on 1 November; next morning they began a forced march that took them by nightfall to a position along the beach east of the Metapona River, where they dug in.

That night, the Japanese succeeded in landing an infantry battalion in the area, their mission being to make contact with surviving Japanese and explore the possibility of establishing an airfield in the region. Torrential rain began to fall, and this put the Marines' radios out of action, so Hanneken had no way to alert his superiors at the Lunga Perimeter of the Japanese landing in the area.

The battle began at daybreak the next day, 3 November, when a Japanese patrol blundered into the Marine lines. Initially the Japanese did not respond aggressively, but once they had recovered their composure they began to bombard Hanneken's battalion with heavy and accurate artillery fire.

With his communications still inoperable and having no supporting arms at his disposal, Hanneken fought a withdrawing action. He took up a position on the other side of the Metapona River, which was to his rear. Despite the fact that this move had to be made in full view of the attacking Japanese it was successfully executed, and a new defensive line was established. But before the situation could be stabilized a small force of Japanese, which had been landed the previous night, struck Hanneken from the rear. About that time, communications were briefly re-established by the Marines, and word was sent back about their predicament to the Division command post.

There were three events occupying their attention: the attack west of the Matanikau by 5th Marines, Hanneken's predicament, and the landing of a Marine reconnaissance force at Aola for airfield survey. To relieve the pressure on Hanneken, General Vandegrift reinforced him with the 1st Battalion, 7th Marines, plus the command element of the 7th Marines, and sent in an air strike. This, however, went horribly wrong, the aircraft bombing and strafing Hanneken's Battalion in error.

Meanwhile Hanneken had not been idle. He launched an attack against the Japanese force to his rear then fell back again to establish a position west of the Nalimbu River. With the assistance of Marine artillery and naval gunfire, Hanneken held. He then established a small beachhead, which was used to land the command element of 7th Marine Regiment, along with the 1st Battalion, 7th Marines, under Puller.

On 4 November, both battalions began an eastward advance under the cover of artillery and naval gunfire. Their action was reinforced by the Army's 164th Infantry (minus its 1st Battalion). Overall command of the operation was placed under General Rupertus, the Assistant Division Commander, 1st Marine Division.

On 6-7 November, after a difficult movement through the jungle, the 164th Regiment linked up with the Marines. The combined forces then advanced eastward. No resistance was met as the Japanese took up a position east of the Metapona River to permit their main force to escape.

By 9 November, the combined American forces had located the Japanese once again and began to surround them. Over the next few days all Japanese attempts to break out were foiled, and the Marines and soldiers, supported by artillery, began to reduce the pocket. By 12 November, they had completed their mission. In this final eastern action, the Americans had lost 40 killed and 120 wounded; the Japanese lost more than 450 killed.

The Aola Operation

In order to cut off any Japanese forces that managed to escape, General Vandegrift asked Admiral Turner to release operational control of

This US Army Private attaches an M1905 bayonet to his M1 Garand rifle. In the latter stages of the campaign, including the battle for the Gifu, the Army provided the bulk of the forces, although a large portion of the 2nd Marine Division was still present. (Shirley Mallinson)

the 2nd Raider Battalion, which Turner had been holding in reserve for another operation. They were landed at Aola to conduct an epic long range patrol from that region to the Mount Austen area. The patrol started out on 5 November. Their main mission was to patrol the Mount Austen area aggressively, destroying any long range artillery that they could locate; in addition, they were to locate and patrol suspected trails leading from the south over Mount Austen and any trails leading from Mount Austen to Kokumbona. Cargo planes from Henderson Field would make periodic supply runs to resupply them. Over the next thirty days the Raiders destroyed numerous artillery pieces and killed 488 Japanese at the cost of 16 killed and 18 wounded, but they were unable to locate any of the suspected trail systems and entered the Lunga Perimeter on 4 December.

The Second Naval Battle For Guadalcanal

After reorganizing their naval forces, the Japanese began to prepare for another reinforcing naval operation. In this Second Naval Battle for Guadalcanal, Admiral Halsey directed Rear Admiral Willis A. 'Ching' Lee to take his battleships, *Washington* and *South Dakota*, and four destroyers to intercept the Japanese. The two forces made contact and in a sharp naval engagement the Japanese were turned back.

The Battle of Tassafaronga

The last naval action in November was the Battle of Tassafaronga. Attempting to resupply the Japanese forces, a 'Tokyo Express' destroyer force was organized for a fast run. Supplies sealed in waterproof drums would be dropped off the destroyers as they ran parallel to the Japanese lines, it being left to the tide to then wash the drums ashore. In the event only a third of the supplies actually reached the Japanese troops and Admiral Tanaka was intercepted by an American task force commanded by Rear Admiral Carleton H. Wright. In the ensuing battle, in which each side lost a destroyer, the Japanese were again turned back. With the close of the month of November, the Japanese no longer enjoyed control of the waters surrounding Guadalcanal.

▲The men of the 2nd Raider Battalion landed at Aola Bay in early November 1942. Part of their mission was to cut off any Japanese stragglers in the area and patrol west to Mount Austen. Here, part of the 2nd Raider Battalion (also known as Carlson's Raiders) assisted by Solomon Islanders crosses an open grassy plain in the Koli Point region. (USMC 51729)

▼The 2nd Raider Battalion continued west until it reached Mount Austen. The battalion was to search for a trail from the south to the summit of Mount Austen. It was also to look for a connecting trail leading to Kokumbona. Here members of the Raider Battalion begin to move up the foothills into the Mount Austen area. (USMC 51728)

THE ARMY TAKES OVER

December saw some definitive changes in the campaign. The Lunga Perimeter was not much larger than it had been in the early days, but there were now enough troops to take decisive offensive action. The American Army was ashore in force, and was led by Major General Patch, who had the AMERICAL Division under his command. This was a unique division in that it had been formed entirely outside the United States, its name being a contracted form of 'America' and 'New Caledonia'.

With Admiral Halsey in overall command, the bleak days were ending. Troops and equipment were pouring into Guadalcanal, and some of the worst-hit Marine units had been relieved and given a much needed rest. Meanwhile the new Army P-38 fighter aircraft was making its début in the area, and B-17 bombers were now based at Henderson Field. And with the tide of war turning it was decided to relieve General Vandegrift's 1st Marine Division. On 9 December, after more than four months of protracted combat, the Marines were pulled out. Sick, tired, dirty and exhausted, they were glad to leave their island purgatory. Command of the ground forces was now turned over to General Patch of the Army, who was left with an experienced cadre of troops, for he still had a major portion of the 2nd Marine Division in his command. This gave him a well balanced force, elements of that division having been on Guadalcanal from the first days. There were also experienced Army and National Guard units ashore.

Intelligence reports indicated that 25,000 Japanese were still on the island – in comparison with 40,000 Americans. However, the exact disposition of the Japanese forces was not known, although it was generally assumed that they were in the Mount Austen and Kokumbona area, and were still being resupplied by the 'Tokyo Express'.

The American objective selected for December was Mount Austen. General Vandegrift had originally planned to capture and incorporate it into the Lunga Perimeter but had changed his plans because of its distance and the limitations of his manpower. Nevertheless, the Army planners deemed Henderson Field would never be secure unless Mount Austen were captured, and it would also need to be secured if the Matanikau region were to be brought completely under American control. A key terrain feature in the fighting Mount Austen is not a single hill mass, but a spur of Guadalcanal's main mountain range. Jutting northward, it dominates the area between the Matanikau and Lunga Rivers. Its 1,514-foot summit is about six miles south-west of Henderson Field and would afford a commanding view of the airfield. Rather than a single peak, it is a series of jungle ridges, a dense rain forest covering the top and waist-high grass over much of the foothills.

It was in this foreboding terrain that Colonel Oka set up his defensive position – a line around Mount Austen's slopes. His force comprised the 124th and 128th Infantry and the 10th Mountain Artillery Regiments.

For the American soldiers who would have to fight there, Mount Austen was a jungle nightmare. Supplies had to be manpacked up the steep slopes and casualties evacuated back the same way. There were no trails – they would come later, eventually being widened to accommodate jeeps, which could assist with resupply and evacuation. But by then the battle would have shifted and the process started all over again.

The fighting was fierce, and the Japanese were well dug in. The attack, which began on 17 December 1942, was not over until 23 January 1943. American soldiers of the 132nd Infantry, which bore the brunt of the fighting, were engaged in a series of battles along the northern ridges. Attacking from east to west, they were eventually halted by the strongest Japanese position, the Gifu

▶ *Conditions on Guadalcanal were certainly not luxurious, and shelter was a combination of what could be found. This picture shows a bomb-proof dugout in front of a lean-to. Note the ample use of captured Japanese rice bags. (USMC 61519)*

which was commanded by Major Takeyoso Inagaki of the 2nd Battalion, 228th Infantry Regiment.

Named after a prefecture in Honshu, Japan, the Gifu was on the western slope of Mount Austen. The strongest part was a horseshoe shaped line, which ran just below the summit. In a series of interconnecting and mutually supporting pillboxes, the Japanese were able to put up an effective resist to the Americans. Initially, the Gifu was difficult to pinpoint. Its north-west boundary was known to the soldiers of the 132nd Infantry only after they had stumbled into the carefully prepared Japanese fields of fire. For days the extent of the position was unknown, and it seemed impossible to outflank until a patrol moving to the south-west through almost impenetrable jungle was able to fix its south-western edge.

By this time, however, hard hit by fatigue and illness and after 22 days of intense jungle warfare, the soldiers of the 132nd Infantry were incapable of further offensive action. (They had lost 112 killed, 268 wounded and three missing; the Japanese had lost about 450 killed.) So, with the 132nd Infantry ringing in the Gifu, the month of December ended. On 4 January 1943, soldiers of the 2nd Battalion, 35th Infantry relieved them, and with the arrival of these fresh troops a new offensive could be mounted.

The January Offensive

With the start of the New Year, General Patch, now commanding XIV Corps, (Americal Division, 25th Infantry Division, 43rd Infantry Division and 2nd Marine Division), resolved to bring matters to a close and drive the Japanese from Guadalcanal: in a series of quick offensive actions, he decided to drive westwards and crush Japanese resistance between Point Cruz and Kokumbona.

The 25th Infantry Division, under the command of Major General J. Lawton Collins, was to sweep the hills overlooking the coast. At the same time, the 2nd Marine Division, commanded by Brigadier General Alphonse De Carre, the Assistant Division Commander, would sweep the coastal area. The 25th Infantry Division, minus the 35th Infantry, in a four day operation cleared out a stubborn Japanese strongpoint west of the Matanikau River in a series of hills known as the 'Galloping Horse', as it bore a resemblance to one from the air. With the clearing of these hills the southern flank was secure for the 2nd Marine Division to attack along the coast.

The 2nd Marine Division, holding a line at Point Cruz, remained in place for the first three days of the 25th Infantry Division's southern operation. On the fourth day, 12 January, it launched a supported offensive against the Japan-

THE JANUARY OFFENSIVE

Clearing the slopes of Mount Austen and the Matanikau sector

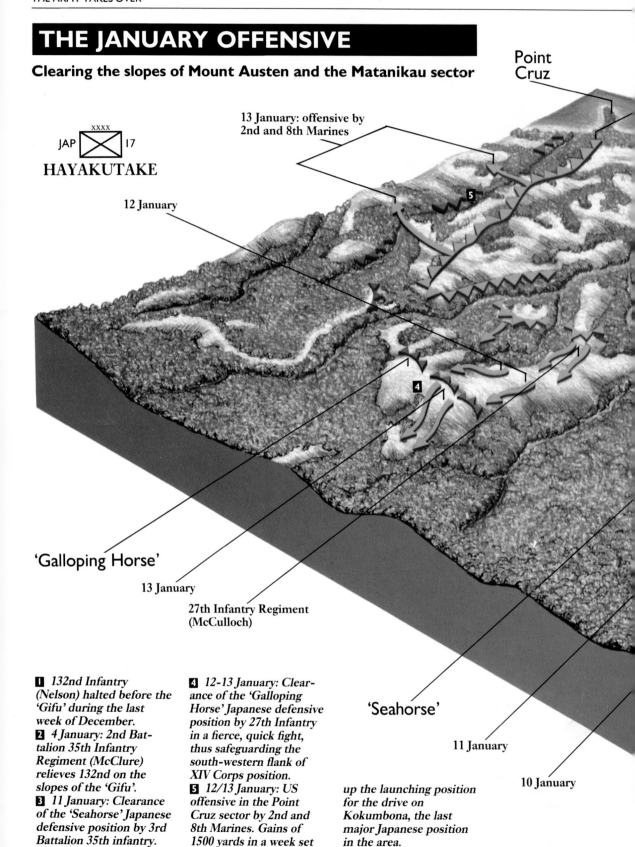

Point Cruz

13 January: offensive by 2nd and 8th Marines

JAP XXXX 17
HAYAKUTAKE

12 January

'Galloping Horse'

13 January

27th Infantry Regiment (McCulloch)

'Seahorse'

11 January

10 January

1 132nd Infantry (Nelson) halted before the 'Gifu' during the last week of December.
2 4 January: 2nd Battalion 35th Infantry Regiment (McClure) relieves 132nd on the slopes of the 'Gifu'.
3 11 January: Clearance of the 'Seahorse' Japanese defensive position by 3rd Battalion 35th infantry.

4 12-13 January: Clearance of the 'Galloping Horse' Japanese defensive position by 27th Infantry in a fierce, quick fight, thus safeguarding the south-western flank of XIV Corps position.
5 12/13 January: US offensive in the Point Cruz sector by 2nd and 8th Marines. Gains of 1500 yards in a week set

up the launching position for the drive on Kokumbona, the last major Japanese position in the area.

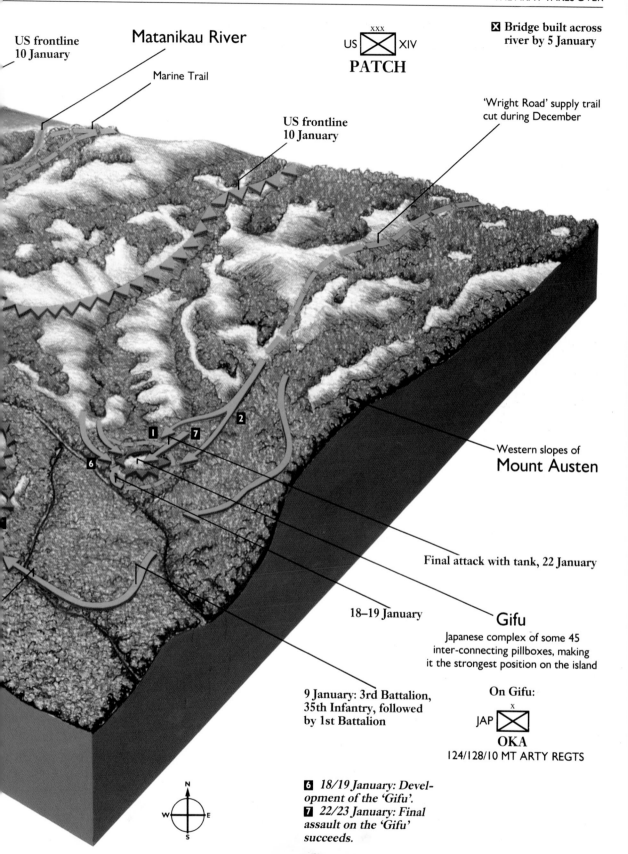

US frontline
10 January

Matanikau River

Marine Trail

US
XXX
XIV
PATCH

☒ Bridge built across
river by 5 January

US frontline
10 January

'Wright Road' supply trail
cut during December

2

1 7

6

Western slopes of
Mount Austen

Final attack with tank, 22 January

18–19 January

Gifu
Japanese complex of some 45
inter-connecting pillboxes, making
it the strongest position on the island

9 January: 3rd Battalion,
35th Infantry, followed
by 1st Battalion

On Gifu:

JAP
X
OKA
124/128/10 MT ARTY REGTS

6 *18/19 January: Devel-
opment of the 'Gifu'.*
7 *22/23 January: Final
assault on the 'Gifu'
succeeds.*

N
W E
S

ese 2nd (Sendai) Division holding the Point Cruz sector. In a one week period the Marines advanced more than 1,500 yards to a position from which a Kokumbona offensive could be launched. In the process they killed an estimated 650 Japanese.

While these gains were being made, the 35th Infantry was engaged in heavy fighting at the Gifu, on Mount Austen, and in the hilly jungle area to the south-west centring on a feature known as the 'Seahorse', from its resemblance in an aerial photograph. In a difficult one day battle the 3rd Battalion, 35th Infantry, seized the 'Seahorse', effectively encircling the Gifu.

Reduction of The Gifu

With the 'Seahorse' thus secured, the difficult task of reducing the Gifu fell to the 2nd Battalion, 35th Infantry. The battle lasted two weeks and was fought against Japanese who were determined to fight to the death. Early in the battle it was realized that tank support would be essential, but none was made available until the end of the operation. Advances were usually made in 100 yard increments. So well were the Japanese concealed that it was often difficult to locate their main line of resistance. Time and time again companies moved up only to be pushed back.

The double envelopment attack was launched on 18-19 January. Gradually resistance began to slacken, and on 22-23 January, three Marine tanks with Army crews were sent to assist in the fighting. Two of them broke down en route; the third pressed on.

In a hellish battle in the jungle, the lone tank supported by sixteen infantrymen penetrated to the heart of the Gifu and then began a systematic destruction of pillboxes and Japanese soldiers. By the night of 22/23 January, the Gifu was quiet. Later that night, the Japanese under Major Inagaki launched an attack to the north-east, but by then the outcome was inevitable, and after a short fight Inagaki and his soldiers were all killed. The reduction of the Gifu had cost the Americans 64 killed and 42 wounded; the Japanese had lost more than 500 killed. Resistance east of the Matanikau River ceased.

With the capture of 'Galloping Horse', the 'Seahorse' and the Gifu, the 25th Infantry Division was able to clear the remaining hills on the southern flank and begin the drive to Kokumbona. In a final two day offensive that ended on 24 January 1943, Kokumbona was captured by the 27th Infantry and the Japanese were driven out of the region. At the end of January, the final task facing XIV Corps was that of pursuing and destroying the Japanese before they could dig in or escape.

◀ *In December 1942, the 2nd Marine Division, as part of General Patch's XIV Corps, made a bold push into the Point Cruz area. This is a forward observation team positioned on a hill overlooking Point Cruz, which is jutting off into the background of this picture. (USMC 53451)*

As the 2nd Marine Division began its drive toward Kokumbona, it ran into periodic pockets of Japanese resistance. Here Marines carry off one of their wounded, as a 37mm anti-tank gun crew take cover behind their gun and jeep. (USMC 53449)

▼ *Below left: A Japanese anti-aircraft gun captured in the drive to Kokumbona. Kokumbona was an important Japanese base camp. It was a trail junction and sat in an ideal, covered bay in which supplies could easily be landed. Its capture was a heavy blow to the Japanese who were now starting to retreat to the west. (USMC 53428)*

Below right: As the 2nd Marine Division began to pursue the retreating Japanese along the coast, they erected bridges by 'field expedient' means. These Marines are crossing the Bonegi River on crude log bridges. (USMC 53424)

THE FINAL PHASE

By the first week of February 1943, Admiral Halsey had been led to expect the Japanese to make another full scale offensive – all intelligence reports pointed to an all-out Japanese effort in the region. But American intelligence had been deceived by the Japanese. After repeated failed offensives, the Japanese had decided to withdraw. To deceive the Americans, and to give the impression that they were preparing for a major offensive, they increased their activities in the area while in reality preparing to evacuate their remaining troops from Doma Cove in the Cape Esperance area. To cover this withdrawal, the Japanese placed 600 troops ashore near Cape Esperance on 14 January, and an additional force landed for a short time in the Russell Islands just to the northwest of Guadalcanal. The Japanese plan called for night withdrawal by destroyer transport, but in the event this was not possible. Barges were to be used to transport the troops to the Russells, where they would be picked up and then taken north.

The Final Push

XIV Corps reached the Poha River on 25 January. Now the campaign began to enter its final stage. A field order was issued directing a combined Army Marine Division (CAM) to attack west on 26 January at 0630; the 6th Marines would move along the northern or beach flank while the 182nd Infantry advanced along the southern, more hilly flank. The 147th Infantry would be in Division reserve, while the American and 25th Division's artillery, along with 2nd Marine Air Wing, would provide direct support for the operation.

The CAM Division's attack began on 26 January and advanced 1,000 yards beyond the Pona River. The Division continued its advance the next day to the Nueha River, where it consolidated its positions.

On 29 January 1943, General Patch detached the 147th Infantry from the CAM Division and reinforced them with artillery from 2nd Battalion, 10th Marines, and 97th Field Artillery Battalion. This composite force was placed under Brigadier General Alphonse De Carre, the Assistant Division Commander, 2nd Marine Division, and was tasked with pursuing the Japanese.

On 30 January at 0700, the 147th Infantry advanced westwards. The supported advance was slowed down by determined Japanese resistance at the Bonegi River. The attack continued the next day, assisted by artillery support. The plan of attack called for the 1st and 2nd Battalions to force a crossing along the coast while the 3rd Battalion would cross inland and capture the ridges to the south, but determined Japanese resistance stalled the coastal advance.

On 1 February 1943, Brigadier General Sebree, Commanding General of the Americal Division, took command of the operation. The attack continued, but so did Japanese resistance, which effectively stopped the Americans. Then on 2 February the Japanese pulled back. It was estimated that 700-800 Japanese had been in the area. Between 3 and 5 February, the Americans advanced west to the Umasani River, meeting no organized resistance.

By early February, General Patch was convinced that the Japanese were no longer going to mount a new offensive. He considered that they were probably planning a withdrawal from Guadalcanal – which he wanted to prevent.

XIV Corps staff had completed plans to land a reinforced battalion on the south-west coast; their mission would be to advance to Cape Esperance and attack the Japanese from the rear, cutting off their escape route. The attack would be led by the 2nd Battalion, 132nd Infantry Regiment under Colonel Alexander M. George. Further consider-

Victory on Guadalcanal, January to February 1943

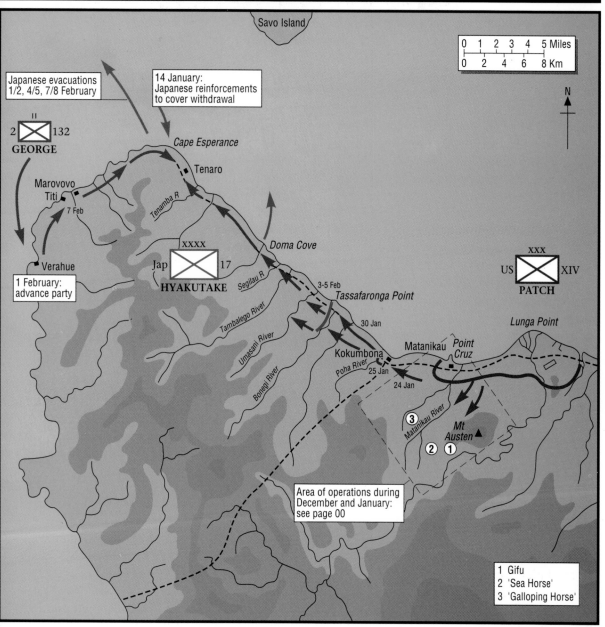

Savo Island

| 0 | 1 | 2 | 3 | 4 | 5 Miles |
| 0 | 2 | 4 | 6 | 8 Km |

N

Japanese evacuations
1/2, 4/5, 7/8 February

14 January:
Japanese reinforcements
to cover withdrawal

2 || 132
GEORGE

Cape Esperance

Tenaro

Marovovo
Titi
7 Feb

Tenamba R

Verahue

1 February:
advance party

XXXX
Jap 17
HYAKUTAKE

Doma Cove

Segilau R

3-5 Feb

XXX
US XIV
PATCH

Tassafaronga Point

Tambalego River

Umasani River

30 Jan

Lunga Point

Kokumbona
Poha River
25 Jan

Matanikau Point
Cruz

Bonegi River

24 Jan

③

Matanikau River

Mt
Austen ▲

② ①

Area of operations during
December and January:
see page 00

1 Gifu
2 'Sea Horse'
3 'Galloping Horse'

ation led to the conclusion that the reinforced battalion might not be sufficiently strong enough to land should there be heavy Japanese opposition, so a small reconnaissance force would land first and set up an advanced post at Titi to determine the strength of the Japanese. This was accomplished in a shore to shore landing on 1 February. Once ashore, the force made effective an reconnaissance of the entire area and recommended that

the battalion be landed at Verahue then move toward Titi.

On 2 February Colonel George's battalion began its advance. Two days later it linked up with the reconnaissance force at Titi, then continued its advance. By 7 February it had reached Marovovo where it settled in for the night.

The movement to Marovovo had been somewhat constrained by a lack of accurate information about the Japanese in the area, and during the day Colonel George had been wounded in the leg. General Patch, who wanted the operation speeded up, sent Colonel Gavan to the battalion's position; but once there he concluded that the operation was progressing satisfactorily and had Colonel George evacuated by boat.

Meanwhile, back at the north coast, General Patch relieved the under-strength 147th Infantry Regiment and ordered the 161st Infantry of the 25th Division (Reinforced), to continue pursuit of the Japanese. Both forces continued their respective advances, meeting only minimal resistance. On 9 February, they met at Tenaro village, and the campaign was now officially over. But 13,000 Japanese had escaped Guadalcanal: the American pincer plan, although excellent in conception, had been executed too slowly.

Indeed, the Japanese had fought a calculated delaying action throughout the final phase, which had begun on 12 January when the Japanese high command issued orders for the withdrawal. Staff officers boarded a destroyer and landed on Guadalcanal. There they proceeded to Seventeenth Army Headquarters and informed General Hyakutake of his new instructions on 15 January. Explaining this new plan to his troops as a change in disposition due to an upcoming future operation, Hyakutake then ordered a withdrawal of Seventeenth Army to Cape Esperance on 22-23 January 1943. The rescuing destroyers made three runs and evacuated the troops during the nights of 1/2, 4/5 and 7/8 February; they were then evacuated to Buin and Rabaul.

The Japanese in the end had been skilful and cunning. Nevertheless the essential significance of the campaign was unchanged. The first phase of the Solomons campaign was concluded as a victory for the Americans, and the first major step had been taken in the reduction of Rabaul.

EPILOGUE

Guadalcanal provided an archetype for jungle and naval warfare in the Pacific. A hard fought campaign that shattered the myth of Japanese invincibility, it was certainly a campaign played out daily in the American press. For months it was a touch and go operation, and there was a national sigh of relief when the Japanese finally withdrew.

From the campaign a seasoned fighting force was created. Veterans came back to teach new replacement troops or stayed on to bolster the ranks of the newly formed units that would carry on the fighting. Most important, the campaign validated the theories and practice of amphibious warfare that had been taught at the Marine Corps schools at Quantico, Virginia, in the late 1920s and 1930s. The concept, though not unique, was certainly not well received in certain military circles – mainly because of memories of the failed attempt at Gallipoli, on the coast of Turkey, in the First World War.

The important gain for the Americans was Guadalcanal itself. It would be developed into one of the largest advanced naval and air bases in the region and would be a springboard for future amphibious operations in the region. And by holding it the Americans had kept open the lines of communication with Australia.

The cost of the campaign had not been prohibitive for the Americans. Total Army and Marine losses were 1,600 killed and 4,700 wounded. The Japanese lost considerably more: 25,400 from all services. Naval losses were more even with each side losing about 25 major warships.

◄ Once the island was secured, it became a staging area for operations up in the northern Solomons. Henderson Field became an important air base for the region. In this picture the original fighter strip has been improved and expanded into a larger bomber strip with taxiways and hard stands. (USMC 108690)

► This is Fighter Strip No 2, located west of the Lunga River. It was constructed to alleviate aircraft congestion at the Henderson Field complex. It was from this fighter strip, that the P-38 fighter planes that shot down Admiral Yamamoto on 18 April 1943 took off. (Signal Corps 171861)

THE BATTLEFIELD TODAY

Guadalcanal has taken many modern steps forward since the Second World War, though it retains many of its past links. It is no longer the remote country it once was but has become a new, emerging nation that is enjoying self-rule.

The most noticeable political change since the war is that the seat of government has moved from Tulagi. It is now located in Honiara, the new capital city on Guadalcanal. Honiara stretches roughly from the Matanikau River west beyond Point Cruz, an area where some of the heaviest fighting occurred.

From the Fiji Islands, Guadalcanal is only a short aircraft flight to Henderson Airport (not the original, but very close to its site). After leaving the aircraft one of the first sights you see as you look west is Mount Austen. With its dominating height, it is not hard to determine why it played such a critical role in the campaign.

The primary area of interest to the historian will, of course, be the battlefields. When touring the battlefields, it is best to rent a four-wheel drive vehicle and hire a local guide. This saves time, money and a lot of frustration. The landing beaches, Alligator Creek, Henderson Field, and 'Bloody Ridge' are all in close proximity and can easily be seen in a day. Mount Austen and the Gifu, although farther away, make for a pleasant drive and tour. From Mount Austen, you get more of a Japanese perspective of the campaign. Some of the other battlefields, such as 'Galloping Horse' and the 'Seahorse', are some distance inland and require proper acclimatization and physical endurance to get to. They are best not tackled alone. An easy way to see them and other remote sites is by charter helicopter.

For the scuba diver, the offshore waters have a variety of ships and planes to dive on. The major warships are down in water too deep to dive safely, but the transports beached and sunk in the November battle are all accessible.

Other areas of interest are Tulagi, Gavutu and Tanambogo. These areas are not often visited and it is wise to coordinate travel and lodging beforehand. There is an abundance of historical wrecks in the area, and these are accessible only by small boat. Most notable is *Kikutsuki*, a Japanese destroyer sunk by pilots from *Yorktown* on 4 May 1942 during a raid made as part of the Battle of the Coral Sea. Later the 34th SeaBees raised the ship, utilizing it as a floating dry dock.

For more detailed information contact the Guadalcanal Tourist Authority, Honiara, Solomon Islands.

CHRONOLOGY

3 May 1942: The 3rd Kure Special Naval Landing Force invades and captures Tulagi, the seat of British Government in the Solomon Islands. They also capture Gavutu, the headquarters for Lever Brothers.

4 May: American carrier planes from *Yorktown* and *Enterprise* make a raid on shipping in Tulagi Harbour, as part of the Battle of the Coral Sea.

8 May: Japanese forces are defeated in the Battle of the Coral Sea. The Japanese invasion forces bound for New Guinea are turned back.

3-4 June: The Americans achieve a strategic victory in the Battle of Midway Island.

8 June: General MacArthur suggests to General Marshall (Army Chief of Staff) that an offensive be taken with New Britain, New Ireland and New Guinea as the objective. MacArthur would be in command.

12 June: General Marshall meets with Admiral King (Chief of Naval Operations) and attempts to foster MacArthur's plan.

14 June: Advance elements of the US 1st Marine Division land in Wellington, New Zealand. They are not expected to see combat until after January.

25 June: Admiral King, after studying the Army plan, rejects it as too ambitious and suggests that the Solomon Islands and Santa Cruz Island be taken first, then New Britain, New Ireland and New Guinea. Admiral Nimitz would be in command.

26 June: General Marshall and Admiral King cannot come to agreement on an offensive plan. King, fearing delays, orders Admiral Nimitz to begin planning to retake the Solomon Islands. Nimitz alerts Vice Admiral Ghormley.

26 June: Admiral Ghormley calls General Vandegrift, the Commanding General of 1st Marine Division to Auckland to announce to him that his division will lead an amphibious assault in the Solomon Islands on 1 August.

29 June to 2 July: General Marshall and Admiral King continue to debate the strategic plan and its commander.

2 July: General Marshall and Admiral King reach an agreement and sign the 'Joint Directive for Offensive Operations in the Southwest Pacific Area Agreed on by the United States Chief of Staff'.

6 July: The Japanese send a survey party to Guadalcanal to select the site for an airfield on the north coast plain. A site is selected near Lunga Point and construction begins. Mid-August is the estimated completion date.

7 July: Vice Admiral Ghormley is selected to command the Guadalcanal–Tulagi amphibious invasion.

11 July: The remainder of the 1st Marine Division reinforced arrives in Wellington, New Zealand.

22 July: The amphibious force sails from New Zealand for the Solomons. The invasion date has been postponed to 7 August.

28-31 July: An amphibious rehearsal is conducted at Koro in a remote area of the Fiji Islands.

7 August: The amphibious force conducts an assault on Guadalcanal, Tulagi, Gavutu and surrounding islands. Tulagi and Gavutu are opposed landings; Guadalcanal is not.

8 August: The Japanese airfield is seized and named Henderson Field in honour of a Marine pilot killed at Midway.

9 August: The Battle for Savo Island. A Japanese naval force under Admiral Mikawa surprises an American naval force near Savo Island. The Americans lose four cruisers sunk and one damaged. The Japanese depart the area with damage to one destroyer. The overall result is that the American Navy departs area, leaving Marines on shore unsupported.

19 August: First Battle of the Matanikau. Battalion sized operation. One company proceeds west along the coast to fix the Japanese at mouth of the river while a second company lands to the west to cut off retreating Japanese. A third company launches the main attack from jungle to the south.

21 August: Battle of the Tenaru. 900 Japanese under Colonel Ichiki attack 2nd Battalion, 1st Marines, at 'Alligator Creek'. In the ensuing action, Colonel Ichiki and his troops are defeated.

24 August: Battle of the Eastern Solomons. A Japanese attempt to reinforce Guadalcanal and block American interdiction of their naval forces. It is not a decisive naval battle, but the Japanese are pulled back.

8 September: Tasimboko Raid. Raiders and Parachutists strike the rear party of the Kawaguchi Brigade, destroying the Japanese supplies. The Marine force narrowly averts destruction by the timely arrival of supply ships mistaken by the Japanese as a reinforcing invasion force.

12-14 September: The Battle of 'Bloody Ridge'. The Japanese under Major General Kawaguchi initiate a three-pronged attack to retake Henderson Field. The attacks are disjointed and unsuccessful. The main attack is launched from the jungle south of a series of ridges south of Henderson Field; the two other attacks strike the Lunga Perimeter from the east and west.

23 September to 9 October: General Vandegrift initiates three operations to expand the Lunga Perimeter by attempting to push the Japanese from Matinkau; but the Japanese hold on the area proves too strong.

11 October: Battle of Cape Esperance. Mutual attempts to land reinforcements lead to a naval clash near Savo Island. The American Navy crosses the 'T' on the Japanese. The naval balance of power begins to shift toward the Americans.

23-26 October: Battle for Henderson Field. Major Japanese air-land-sea offensive. A three-pronged attack is planned, but attacks are not coordinated and are unsupported. The Japanese are defeated.

26 October: Battle of the Santa Cruz Islands. A Japanese victory by naval forces supporting the land operation.

12-13 November: First Naval Battle of Guadalcanal. An American cruiser force intercepts a Japanese battleship force. In the ensuing battle, Admirals Scott and Callaghan are killed, but the Japanese are turned back.

14-15 November: Second Naval Battle for Guadalcanal. American battleships turn back a Japanese naval force.

1-4 November: American western offensive. Elements of the 1st Marines cross the Matankau and push past Point Cruz.

2-3 November: American eastern offensive. Elements of the 7th Marines push the Japanese out of the Koli Point area.

5 November to 4 December: 2nd Raider Battalion ('Carlson's Raiders') conducts a historic patrol from Aola to Mount Austen.

30 November: Battle for Tassafaronga. A Japanese destroyer force dropping off supplies is driven away by American forces.

9 December: 1st Marine Division is relieved and sails from Guadalcanal.

15 December 1942 to 26 January 1943: The American Army engages in a bitter fight to drive the Japanese from the Mount Austen area.

13-17 January: The 2nd Marine Division launches an offensive that pushes the Japanese from the Point Cruz area.

22-3 January: The westward push continues and the Japanese are driven out of Kokumbona area.

1-8 February: The Japanese withdraw from Doma Cove on destroyers.

9 February 1943: Guadalcanal is secured by the Americans.

A GUIDE TO FURTHER READING

There is no single definitive book on the Guadalcanal campaign, although there are many claims to that effect. To assist the serious student of the campaign, many primary source books are listed below. This list in itself is not a complete one, but it covers the major works.

Coggins, Jack. *The Campaign for Guadalcanal*. New York, Doubleday and Company, 1972.

Craven, Wesley Frank and Cates, James Lea (eds). *The Pacific: Guadalcanal to Saipan. August 1942 to July 1944 – The Army Air Forces in World War II*, vol. 4. Chicago, University of Chicago Press, 1950. pp. 37-60.

Frank, Richard B. *Guadalcanal: The Definitive Account of the Land Battle*. Random House, New York, 1990, VII–800.

Ferguson, Robert Lawrence. *Guadalcanal, Island of Fire; Reflections of the 347th Fighter Group*. Tab Books, Blue Ridge Summit, 1987. VII–256.

Guadalcanal: Island Ordeal, Ballantine Books, Inc., New York 1971.

Guadalcanal Remembered. Doddimead & Company, New York 1982. V-332.

Hammel, Eric. *Guadalcanal: Starvation Island*. Crown Publishers, Inc, New York. V-478.

Hammel, Eric. *Guadalcanal, The Carrier Battles*. Crown Publishers, Inc., New York. V-505.

— *Guadalcanal, Decision at Sea*. Crown Publishers, Inc., New York. V-480.

Hough, Frank O., Lt Col USMCR, and Ludwig, Verle E., Maj USMC, and Shaw, Henry I., Jr. *Pearl Harbor to Guadalcanal – History of US Marine Corps Operations in World War II*, vol. 1. Washington, Historical Branch, G-3 Division, Headquarters, US Marine Corps, 1958. pp. 235-74.

Hoyt, Edwin P. *Guadalcanal*. Military Heritage Press, 1988. 1-322.

Isley, Jeter A. and Crowl, Philip A. *The US Marines and Amphibious War*. Princeton, Princeton University Press, 1951. pp. 72-165.

Johnston, Richard W. *Follow Me! The Story of the Second Marine Division in World War II*. New York, Random House, 1948. pp. 24-81.

Kilpatrick, C. W. *The Naval Night Battles in the Solomons*. Exposition Press of Florida, Inc., Pompano Beach, 1986. 1-170.

Leckie, Robert. *Challenge for the Pacific*. Doubleday and Company, Inc., New York, 1965. VII-372.

Edward, Lee Robert. *Victory at Guadalcanal*. Presidio Press, Novato, 1981. V-260.

McMillan, George. *The Old Breed: A History of the First Marine Division in World War II*. Washington, Infantry Journal Press, 1949. pp. 25–142.

Merillat, Herbert C., Capt USMCR. *The Island: A History of the Marines on Guadalcanal*. Houghton Mifflin Company, Boston 1944. VII-283.

Miller, John, Jr. *Guadalcanal: The First Offensive – The War in the Pacific – United States Army in World War II*. Washington, Historical Division, Department of the Army, 1949. xviii-413.

Morison, Samuel Eliot. *The Struggle for Guadalcanal – History of United States Naval Operations in World War II*. vol. v. Boston: Little, Brown and Company, 1950. xxii, 389 pp.

Sherrod, Robert. *History of Marine Corps Aviation in World War II*. Washington, Combat Forces Press, 1952. pp. 65-129.

Stone, John Scott. *Iron Bottom Bay*. Stone Enterprises, Pivarr, Texas, 1985. 1-384.

Tregreskis, Richard. *Guadalcanal Diary*. Random House, New York, 1943. 1-263.

Zimmerman, John L., Maj USMCR. *The Guadalcanal Campaign*. Washington, Historical Division, Headquarters, US Marine Corps, 1949. vi-189.

WARGAMING GUADALCANAL

Unlike the German invasion of France, the North African Campaign, the war on the Eastern Front or the Normandy Campaign, the land battles fought in the Pacific have not attracted the attention of many wargamers. Despite the existence of several very attractive ranges of wargames figures and vehicles, in a wide variety of scales ranging from 1:72 to 1:300, the lack of major battles that involve large numbers of armoured vehicles reduces the Pacific war's appeal to many wargamers. The naval aspects of the Pacific war have also tended to be ignored as a subject for wargamers. Most naval wargamers find that, as the major battles such as the Coral Sea and Midway are dominated by aircraft carriers and their planes, and that the best way to recreate these battles seems to be as board or map games, they do not have the opportunity to fight ship-to-ship actions in which gunfire predominates.

As this book shows, the Guadalcanal Campaign has much to offer the wargamer who wishes to try something new. It would make an excellent basis for a club campaign, particularly as, unlike the later battles in the Pacific war, the outcome was by no means a foregone conclusion. Each phase of the campaign could be wargamed in a variety ways, and the participants interest could, therefore, be maintained throughout, thus overcoming the boredom factor which so often afflicts club campaigns. Alternatively, for those who prefer one-off games, each phase of the campaign could be played out as separate but still very interesting games.

The American Invasion Plan

The pre-landing planning carried out by the Americans can best be simulated by adopting the Committee Game format, which has been developed over the years by such groups as Wargame Developments and The Chestnut Lodge Wargames Group. Each of the players is given a role to play (such as General MacArthur, Admiral King, Admiral Nimitz, General Marshall, etc.) and a detailed briefing that outlines the parameters within which they must work, plus any information they would have about the forces available, the enemy's intentions, etc. They then sit down and thrash out a plan of action. As each player will have different 'goals', the Committee Game will throw up many of the problems the real people had to deal with – for example, cooperation between the Army and the Navy, and between the Navy and the Marines.

Once the strategic plans have been formulated, the players can move on to the tactical planning stage. The Committee Game format can again be used, but this time the players will need to take on the roles of the Naval Force Commander and the Marine Divisional, Regimental and Battalion Commanders. A detailed Order of Battle (or Orbat) for the United States Forces involved in the assault will be required, as will a map of the area surrounding Guadalcanal. The players can then begin to plan how to mount an assault on Guadalcanal and the surrounding islands. As you will have already read, for the United States Navy and Marine Corps this was very much a case of learning 'on the job'; so it would be particularly interesting to see how different the plans the players end up developing are from those that were actually put into effect.

The Assault on Guadalcanal and the early Land Battles

Because of the relatively small-scale nature of the initial landings on Tulagi, Gavatu, Tanambogo, Florida Island and Guadalcanal, it is quite possible to recreate these actions using 20mm or 1:76 scale models. Such games have already been popularzed by a group of wargamers from the Grimsby area in England, and their games – such as the one that deals with the Japanese attack upon Wake Island – have been featured in the pages of *Wargames Illustrated* as well as at numerous shows around Great Britain. The Grimsby wargamers use their own wargames rules in their recreations, but several sets of rules exist that would be ideal for refighting the land battles fought on Guadalcanal. In particular, *Command Decision*, which was written by Frank Chadwick and published by Game Designers Workshop, is suitable for games involving division or regiment sized units.

Two areas of amphibious operations not covered by most sets of Second World War wargames rules are Naval Gunfire in support of Land Forces and Shore Battery Gunfire against Landing Craft. In the former instance, this can be simulated by the Naval Commander 'guesstimating' the range, which is then measured and adjusted left or right, and up or down, by the umpire. The umpire 'generates' a degree of error by throwing two D6 dice and reading the result from the following chart.

Dice Score:	Degree of Error:
2	No adjustment
3	Down 100 metres
4	Down 100 metres
5	Down 200 metres
6	Right 100 metres
7	No Adjustment
8	Left 100 metres
9	Up 200 metres
10	Up 100 metres
11	Up 100 metres
12	No adjustment

An alternative method to that outlined above, which uses a small programmable calculator, has been developed by Tim Price of Wargame Developments, and was published in a 1991 issue of *The Nugget*. A similar method can be used to Shore Battery Gunfire, but the problem of how many troops will survive if their Landing Craft is hit and sunk remains. One way in which this can be done is to use the following formula:

$$\frac{100 - \text{Distance from beach (m)}^2}{50^2}$$

This gives the percentage of the troops reaching the beach safely. For example, a landing craft is hit and sunk 200 metres from the beach; therefore 84 per cent of the troops in the landing craft reach the beach safely: a landing craft is hit and sunk 400 metres from the beach; therefore 36 per cent of the troops in the landing craft reach the beach safely.

One of the major problems faced by the United States Marines as they landed on Guadalcanal was the fact that their information about the terrain was faulty. This aspect of the assault can be gamed by adapting the system outlined by Peter Gritton in an early issue of *Wargames Illustrated*. A grid of playing cards is laid out, face down, on a table. As the Marines reach the grid, the card in front of them is turned over and this 'generates' the terrain they are about to enter; for example, the Ace of Clubs means impenetrable bushes; the 8 of Hearts means open terrain; the Queen of Diamonds means a clearing surrounded by trees. This is an excellent way of recreating the uncertainty of advancing in unfamiliar country, and if cards representing Japanese forces are mixed in with terrain cards one can end up with some excellent ambush/counter-attack games involving small forces. This system can also be used to recreate the actions that resulted from the patrols the Americans sent out in the early stages of the campaign.

The Land Battles on Guadalcanal

One of the major attractions to the wargamer in recreating the land battles for Guadalcanal are: first, the varied terrain over which the battles were fought; and, second, the problems of logistics and the health of the troops. The first of these gives wargamers the opportunity to exercise their talents for creating a wide variety of terrain on the table-top – Guadalcanal has swamps, tropical jungle, a coastal plain, steep hills and torrential rivers, all of which will require different methods of warfare as well as affecting the movement of troops.

The solution to the problem of maintaining a constant supply of food and ammunition while at the same time keeping one's troops healthy will be important, as these factors affected the numbers of troops available for action, their capacity to fight and their morale or 'will to combat'. These things are difficult for the wargamer to recreate, but several Second World War wargame rules include sections that can be adapted for use. In particular, *Command Decision* has rules dealing with a lack of ammunition supply and its effects upon a unit's ability to fight; while Chris Kemp's *Not Quite Mechanised* rules are specifically devised to emphasize the problems of logistics on the battlefield and the changes in fighting capacity of troops who have been in battle for any length of time.

The Air War

Many wargamers find this aspect of warfare the most difficult to recreate because it takes place in three dimensions, so it is often either ignored or only appears as a notional factor in land fighting. That said, Mike Spick, the doyen of Air Wargamers, has shown that it is possible to fight one-to-one air battles on the table-top very easily, while other wargamers have achieved very creditable results using a variety of gadgets such as stands, turning circles and firing arcs. Control of the air was an important aspect of the Guadalcanal campaign, and it is therefore vital that the Air War is not ignored if one is recreating the campaign. One method of doing this might be to use one of the board or computer games that recreate aerial combat. Certainly the latter, which happen in 'real-time', give you the flavour of actually flying an aircraft in combat without the danger of risking being killed!

Map and Board Games

For those wargamers who do not have the time or inclination to collect and paint large numbers of model soldiers, tanks or aircraft, or who wish to fight campaigns at a higher level of command than that of a divisional, regimental or battalion commander, the best answer lies in map or board games. The former have a long history going back to the original *Kriegsspiel* of the early nineteenth century, while the latter have their own large and devoted following among the wargaming fraternity. Both are admirable ways of recreating the Guadalcanal campaign, and both have their advantages and disadvantages. In the case of map games, the main disadvantage is in the amount of work the umpire has to do; its main advantage lies in its infinite flexibility. Board games have the advantage that they come, in most cases, 'ready-to-use', and it is possible to get games that deal specifically with the Guadalcanal campaign; their main disadvantage is that they tend to be very specific and are thus somewhat inflexible. They also seem not to have been designed to be played repeatedly, and can sometimes appear to be expensive in relation to the amount of 'game-time' players get out of them. Like so many things in wargaming, one pays one's money and takes one's choice.